D0874347

AN UNLIKELY TRUST

AN UNLIKELY TRUST

ALINA'S STORY OF ADOPTION, COMPLEX TRAUMA, HEALING, AND HOPE

THE ORP LIBRARY

WRITTEN BY

JEFF KRUKAR, PH.D.

KATIE GUTIERREZ

WITH

JAMES G. BALESTRIERI

rtc Publishing

WRITERS OF THE ROUND TABLE PRESS
PO BOX 511
HIGHLAND PARK, IL 60035

Publisher	COREY MICHAEL BLAKE
Executive Editor	KATIE GUTIERREZ
Post Production	DAVID CHARLES COHEN
Directoress of Happiness	ERIN COHEN
Director of Author Services	KRISTIN WESTBERG
Facts Keeper	MIKE WINICOUR
Cover Design	ANALEE PAZ
Interior Design and Layout	SUNNY DIMARTINO
Proofreading	RITA HESS
Last Looks	JESS PLACE
Digital Book Conversion	SUNNY DIMARTINO
Digital Publishing	SUNNY DIMARTINO

Printed in the United States of America
First Edition: May 2013
10 9 8 7 6 5 4 3 2 1

Library of Congress Cataloging-in-Publication Data
Krukar, Jeff
An unlikely trust: alina's story of adoption, complex trauma, healing,
and hope / Jeff Krukar and Katie Gutierrez with James G. Balestrieri.—
1st ed. p. cm.
Print ISBN: 978-1-939418-16-6   Digital ISBN: 978-1-939418-19-7
Library of Congress Control Number: 2013938891
Number 3 in the series: The ORP Library
The ORP Library: An Unlikely Trust

RTC Publishing is an imprint of Writers of the Round Table, Inc.
Writers of the Round Table Press and the RTC Publishing logo
are trademarks of Writers of the Round Table, Inc.

CONTENTS

INTRODUCTION

Today, according to the U.S. Department of Health and Human Services, more than 5.5 million children—or eight percent of kids—in the U.S. have some form of disability. Whether the problem is physical, behavioral, or emotional, these children struggle to communicate, learn, and relate to others. While there is no longer *segregation* in the same sense as there was in the 1950s, what remains the same is the struggle. Even with all of our resources and technology, parents of children with disabilities fight battles every day to find the help and education their children need.

I have led Oconomowoc Residential Programs (ORP) for almost thirty years. We're a family of companies offering specialized services and care for children, adolescents, and adults with disabilities. Too often, when parents of children with disabilities try to find funding for programs like ours, they are bombarded by red tape, conflicting information, or no information at all, so they struggle blindly for years to secure an appropriate education. Meanwhile, home life, and the child's wellbeing, suffers. In cases when parents and caretakers have exhausted their options—and their hope—ORP is here to help. We felt it was time to offer parents a new, unexpected tool to fight back: stories that educate, empower, and inspire.

The original idea was to create a library of comic books that could empower families with information to reclaim their rights. We wanted to give parents and caretakers the information they need to advocate for themselves, as well as provide educators and therapists with a therapeutic tool. And, of course, we wanted to reach the children—to offer them a visual representation of their journey that would show that they aren't alone, nor are they wrong or "bad" for their differences. What we found in the process of writing original stories for the comics is that these journeys are too long, too complex, to be contained within a standard comic. So what we are now creating is an ORP library of disabilities books—traditional books geared toward parents, caretakers, educators, and therapists, *and* comic books portraying the world through the eyes of children with disabilities. Both styles of books share what we have learned while advocating for families over the years while also honestly highlighting their emotional journeys. We're creating communication devices that anyone can read to understand complex disabilities in a new way.

In an ideal situation, these books will be used therapeutically, to communicate the message, and to help support the work ORP and companies like ours are doing. The industry has changed dramatically and is not likely to turn around any time soon—certainly not without more people being aware of families' struggles. We have an opportunity to put a face to the conversation, reach out to families, and start that dialogue.

Caring for children with disabilities consumes your life. We know that. And we want you to realize, through these stories, that you are not alone. We can help.

Sincerely,
Jim Balestrieri
CEO, Oconomowoc Residential Programs
www.orplibrary.com

A NOTE ABOUT THIS BOOK

Complex trauma and reactive attachment disorder are conditions that affect children in different ways. The child depicted in the following story struggles with significant emotional and behavioral difficulties that require short-term placement in a specialized therapeutic environment. Many children with complex trauma do not resemble the child shown in this story. However, those who are similar to Alina face challenges that make it difficult to benefit from special education in a traditional public school setting. Genesee Lake School strives to build relationships with the children in its care so that they learn new skills that will lead to a successful transition back to their homes, schools, and communities. It is our hope that the following story will add to your own understanding of the often lonely journey experienced by families with children with these unique challenges and gifts.

PROLOGUE
PUT THE KNIFE DOWN

"Alina! Alina, honey, it's okay—calm down." Julie Ryan fought the darkness invading her vision. She held her arms out to her daughter, palms upturned. "Honey, just put the knife down. You're going to hurt yourself."

Alina was wild. Her strawberry blond hair swung into her gray-blue eyes, narrowed and mean. She was ten years old but tiny—most people thought she was six or seven—and her limbs were wiry and straining as she bounced her weight from foot to foot, wary as a boxer, dangerous as a snake. No one, not even Julie's husband Mark, could control Alina when she raged like this. Adrenaline and wave after wave of fury made her stronger than any child her size should be. With her back to the open doorway of the kitchen, Alina let out the same throat-ripping shrieks that had made the neighbors twice call the police.

"Honey, it's okay. It's okay. Just let the knife fall to the floor. Do like this." Julie edged closer to Alina, opening and closing her right hand in a pantomime of dropping something.

"No!" Alina's fair skin reddened. She swiped the knife through the air, and Julie stopped.

"Okay. I'm not getting any closer. I'm staying right here. Okay?"

From behind Alina, Mark quietly approached; he'd circled around and entered the kitchen from the laundry room. He looked at Julie—a millisecond glance one cop might give another in a dangerous situation, a quick reminder of partnership—as he snuck toward Alina. His arms were held out at his sides, and the deliberate way he crept forward reminded Julie of a cartoon burglar.

"Alina, we love you." Julie spoke loudly to cover any sound Mark was making. "You know that, right? We love you so much."

Alina, her cheeks scarlet, glared at Julie with blind rage.

Mark lunged. With a grunt, he wrapped his arms around her and pinned hers at her side. He gripped her tiny wrist with his right hand, shaking it, trying to make her drop the knife, but Alina let out another shriek, so long and loud it seemed impossible for her lungs to hold that much breath. Then she threw her head backwards into Mark's face.

"Alina, no!" Julie cried, rushing forward. She joined the fray, trying to pry Alina's fingers from the knife as her daughter screamed and spit.

Mark let out a painful curse as blood rushed from his nose, but he didn't let go.

"Mommy?" The fearful call came from the base of the stairs, where their youngest child, Margaret, stood, clutching a blanket in one hand.

Julie gasped as Alina headbutted her, catching her cheekbone. The darkness in Julie's vision swelled. "Honey, it's okay. Go to your room," she called out to Margaret.

Over Alina's thrashing body, which Julie and Mark could hardly contain, their eyes met again. Blood pooled on his upper lip while sweat made him blink hard. The same desperate question Julie had was reflected in his gaze.

What do we do now?

CHAPTER 1
FIVE YEARS EARLIER

"Mark, it's here! We got it!"

Julie dumped her purse on the kitchen island and dropped the rest of the day's mail beside it. She stared at an envelope from the international adoption agency, her hand shaking as she darted into the hallway.

"Mark? Did you hear me? Come into the kitchen!"

"Mom, why are you yelling?" It was their seven-year-old son, Lucas. He poked his head over the back of the couch in the den, where Julie hadn't even noticed he was laying. "What did we get?"

Julie smiled as she walked over to him, kissing the top of his head. His chestnut hair was rumpled, as if he'd been playing outside. "We got a picture of your sister."

Lucas made a face, but curiosity got the better of him. "I want to see!"

"Hang on, I want to show your dad at the same time. Where is he?"

Lucas jerked his head toward the French doors. "Mowing the lawn."

She pulled open one of the doors and called out to her husband, who was sweating at the helm of their ever-problematic mower. He squinted at her and pulled an earbud from his ear. She just waved the envelope and grinned.

Inside, the three of them crowded together over the island, where they always seemed to gather. "Here we go . . ." Julie said. Carefully, she opened the envelope and pulled out a five by seven photo. Her breath caught, and immediately her eyes rushed with tears. "Alina," she said.

The little girl in the photo was just over three years old. Her light hair was harshly cropped, as if someone had blindly taken a pair of shears to it, and her eyes were wide and serious, staring directly at the camera. She wore a long-sleeved white top beneath a pair of denim overalls, and her hands made tiny fists in her lap.

"Why isn't she smiling?" Lucas asked.

Julie laughed, wiping tears. "You can't make three-year-olds do anything." Her voice was light, but the solemnity of Alina's face tugged at her heart. She wanted to go get her, *now*.

Mark smiled and took Julie's hand. "It's finally happening."

"I know."

Lucas looked between them, his face clouding. "When she comes, are you guys going to love her more than me?"

"Oh, honey!" Julie said at the same time Mark grabbed their son and pulled him close. "There is more than enough love to go around in this family."

• • •

Julie and Mark had met in college at the University of Wisconsin-Madison. They both came from big families, the type that always seemed to be taking in another kid:

a niece or nephew in trouble, their children's friends, anyone who needed a break from their own families for a while. Julie never knew whom she'd see at the dinner table, and Mark kept a sleeping bag in his closet in case someone needed it at the last minute. Though their families weren't perfect, neither could imagine having a small one. They talked early on about the possibility of adoption, confident they would take that path one day.

They married right after graduation, and Julie was pregnant by the end of their honeymoon. Life as a married couple began. Both worked full-time—Mark at a bank's IT department and Julie doing marketing for a museum—and years passed before they caught their breath. When Lucas was four and they started to talk about having another child, suddenly all those conversations about adoption flooded back. Julie lost time in front of the computer, scouring adoption agency sites and reading story after story of kids who needed parents.

"Why have we waited so long?" Julie asked one night. Lucas was in bed, and she and Mark were sharing a bottle of Chianti while digging into calzones. "I mean really. Mark, there are so many kids in this world who don't have a home. In Russia alone, there are seven hundred thousand orphans. Seven hundred thousand! That's more than at the end of World War II, when twenty-five million Russians were killed. How is that even possible these days?"

Mark shook his head. "I don't know," he said. "But Jules, we couldn't exactly do it fresh out of college, or when Lucas was a baby. Are you serious about adopting now?"

Julie nodded. Without realizing it, she'd made up her mind long before this conversation. "Absolutely."

...

The process wasn't simple, nor was it quick. Then again, Julie hadn't expected it to be. International adoption was rife with hurdles and loopholes, laws changing at the last minute and files mysteriously disappearing. But now, supposedly—a year after receiving her photo—they were nine months away from bringing Alina home.

They didn't know much about her. Her profile was sketchy, at best: her mother was seventeen years old, with two other kids by two different fathers, and had aged out of a state-run orphanage. She was an alcoholic, and though Alina wasn't diagnosed with fetal alcohol syndrome, there was enough concern to have her placed in a "baby house" for children with mild to severe disabilities. She'd been taken to the baby house straight from the hospital and had been there ever since. At four, she was underweight, undersized, and showing signs of developmental delays: she had an inconsistent response to sights and sounds, was slow to walk and talk, and was delayed in personal care skills.

When Mark and Julie had been asked by family and friends if they were willing to adopt a child with a disability, they'd had several long, difficult discussions. They had been so blessed with Luke and couldn't imagine the different lives they'd be leading if he were disabled. On the other hand, they hadn't been able to choose whether Luke was healthy or not, and if he were to have been born with a disability, would they love him any less? Would they wish they could send him back? Of course not. Ultimately, they decided that if they were going to adopt, it had to be with the same sense of unconditional

4

love they'd felt the minute Julie found out she was pregnant with Luke.

Finally, nearly two years after receiving Alina's photo and profile, Julie and Mark booked their tickets to Russia. By law, they needed to go twice: the first time to meet her and go to court, and the second to bring her home. When their friends and family asked if they were ready, Julie responded jokingly, "How would you feel being pregnant for two years?" Everyone laughed, but the analogy hit at a deep truth. In many ways, their lives had been in limbo ever since they'd received Alina's picture. In their hearts, she was a part of their family already—she was *theirs*— and yet they couldn't move forward. She was growing older apart from them, and the more time that went by, the more worried they became for her. Was she being properly cared for? Were her basic needs being met? Was she being fed well? Was she receiving lots of nurturing from adults? Did people show care and concern for her? Did she play often with other kids? Once they committed to Alina as a part of their family, trusting her to the care of strangers was just as terrifying and consuming as it would have been to leave Luke at a random doorstep with a note reading, "We'll pick him up in two years." What could happen and who would he become during that time?

"Don't you ever worry," friends asked, "about adopting a child that's already a toddler? It's one thing when they're babies, but when they're older, you just never know. It's harder for older kids to change."

"And from *Russia*, of all places," others added, shuddering. "It's great what you're doing, don't get me wrong, but are you sure you know what you're getting yourselves into? I've heard horror stories about kids adopted from other countries."

Julie and Mark bristled at the questions, but the truth was that neither of them had a real clue what they were getting themselves into. Then again, that was parenthood. The fear, the worry, the joy, the panic, the hope—those emotions vibrated inside them constantly with Luke and did so now with Alina, intensified by uncertainty and anticipation.

...

It was early January, and the Russian city was starkly cold but clear. The skies were bluish gray with low hanging clouds, and the ground was coated in snow. Julie and Mark burrowed into their coats on the ride to the orphanage, wind pressing against the doors and windows as their translator (provided by the international adoption agency) drove. Soon, they would be meeting Alina, their five-year old daughter, for the first time.

"Are you ready for this?" Mark took Julie's hand, but she could barely feel anything through her thick leather gloves.

She kissed his cold cheek. "I already feel like crying. I just know I will."

"I know, honey. I'd be surprised if I didn't."

Once they arrived, they talked briefly through the translator to the orphanage director, who led them down a hallway. The orphanage looked like an old brick school building, faded white, built in the early 1900s. The halls were all gray cinderblock and a tile floor that had seen years of wear. The lighting was inconsistent, with some areas seeming to be more brightly lit than others. While the inside of the building was warmer than outside, Julie realized that she was still shivering as they walked with the orphanage director. The air smelled like a poorly run daycare—the sharp scents of bleach and disinfectant trying to cover more pungent odors. Their booted steps echoed as they walked, and Julie was surprised she didn't hear any children. She squeezed Mark's hand hard, and he gave an understanding squeeze back.

In a small meeting room, they waited with barely contained nerves while a social worker went for Alina. The woman returned ten minutes later, carrying a small child against her shoulder. She smiled at Julie and Mark, saying in crisp English, "Here is Alina." She set Alina down in a chair facing the Ryans, and for a moment, Julie lost her breath. Alina was so *tiny*—Julie hadn't realized quite how small, how completely defenseless, she would seem. The bulkiness of the seat of her pants revealed that she was also still in diapers. She stared at them intensely, her eyes watchful and wary. Then Alina offered a small smile.

"Mama," she said. "Papa."

Julie and Mark laughed with relief, and they both knelt before Alina. She let Julie hug her softly, but her body stiffened and she didn't return the embrace. Julie felt an overwhelming urge to examine her little body for any signs of abuse or mistreatment and whisk her away from there—take her home. But there was a process to follow.

They spent half an hour with her that day, trying to engage her to play with toys from a basket the orphanage director offered. Alina stared at them blankly. When the social worker gave her a banana, she ran into a corner and ate it in a frenzy, watching them the whole time.

The only words she spoke were, "Mama," "Papa," and "no." When Julie and Mark left, they gave the orphanage director a box of clothes, toys, and photos they'd brought for Alina. The clothes were far too big, however, so they promised to send some that were the proper size.

The next day, the agency translator accompanied them to court. Both Julie and Mark were dressed in dark business suits, and they met with a female judge in another small room. The judge's eyes were a vivid blue, and frown lines marked a faint track between her eyebrows. A court reporter occupied a small desk to the left of the judge's bench, and her fingers moved quickly as they talked.

"Tell me, why do you wish to adopt Alina?" the judge asked Mark, whom she had asked to stand first.

"We have one biological child, Lucas, whom we love with all our hearts," Mark said. "We want more children but would prefer, at this point, to give a child without parents a home. We love Alina," he added. "For a long time now, we've considered her our daughter."

"How will you provide for her?"

"Both Julie and I work full-time, though Julie has arranged to take six months off to help Alina adjust when she comes home."

"I've read that you have a son. What does he think of this?"

"Well, he'd have preferred a little brother," Mark tried to joke. The judge was unmoved. "I'm kidding. He's excited to meet his new sister."

The judge continued down a series of questions, and Julie's voice trembled a little when her turn came to answer. She was so ready to end this part of the journey and start the next—life with their son *and* daughter.

They were in Russia for only three days before flying back to the States, jet-lagged and emotionally spent. Their second and final court appointment was scheduled for two months later—on the first day of spring. To the Ryans, this sense of a new beginning seemed like a fitting omen.

CHAPTER 2
THEY'RE GOING TO TORTURE YOU

Everything open. Roar, loud but quiet, like it was in her chest. See-through, cracked open sky, flying. Flying! Clouds, white. She pounded the window. Wanting to touch the clouds! Pounded, she yelled. Lady—Mama—touching. Jumped. Stared. Mama. Papa.

"Honey, shhh. People are trying to sleep."

Shhh. Shhh. Shhh. Sleep. Clattering bars. *Lights out—sleep!* Blackness. Nothing. In blackness, sounds: high, loud, then silence. Laying in her crib. On her back, staring up. Nothing but the ceiling. Black at night. Babies crying all the time. Her crib, she moved. Side, side, side, side, side.

"Honey, are you okay?"

Mama. Mama looking at her. Papa looking at her. The orphanage lady: *Remember—you need to call them Mama and Papa. They're going to take you away to a big house in America.*

The orphanage boys: *They're going to kidnap you. They're going to sell you. They're going to kill you.*

Lady: *You're going to go to a school and will learn English.*

Boys: *They're going to torture you. Hang you from the ceiling and pull off your fingernails.* Screaming, falling to floor.

"Are you hungry, sweetie? Here, why don't we have some apple?"

Mama reaching under the seat. Hand moving in a bag. Sucking sound, apple! Pieces, in a bowl. Apple, it was hers!

"Mine!" she yelled. Grabbed, pulled. Hide, time to hide!

"Alina, it's okay. No one's going to take it from you, I promise!" Papa.

"I wonder if she didn't get enough food at the orphanage?" Mama.

"We'll have to take her to Dr. Prentiss right away." Papa.

"I've already made the appointment. Let's not talk about this in front of her, though."

She ate. Apple, all hers. Sweet and juicy. She ate fast, kept looking at Mama and Papa. *Hers.*

Lights on! She blinked hard. Stared.

"I think that scared her. Mark, turn that light off."

"Why would she be scared of light?"

"I don't know, but she practically leapt out of her seat when you turned it on. Turn it off."

Lights off.

Shh. Shh. Shh. Side, side, side, side, side.

"What's she doing?" Papa.

"She's . . . rocking herself." Mama. "I don't—did Luke ever do that?"

"No, he didn't. Not that I remember."

"Honey?" Gentle voice. Soft. Side, side, side, side, side. "Honey, are you okay? We're here. We're almost home."

CHAPTER 3
CAN YOU SAY "HOME"?

They landed in Milwaukee at four in the afternoon after an exhausting ten-hour flight. Alina didn't sleep at all. The whole time, she either pounded the window or stared, seeming lost in her own thoughts. She watched everyone and everything with a look of intense wariness. The expression was unnerving to Julie. It seemed to belong to someone much older, someone who had been hurt by the world, seen too much. This mistrust was jarring to see in the eyes of an innocent child.

The airport was loud with the hustle of travelers, intercom announcements, and music drifting out of stores. In front of baggage claim, Alina froze at first and then walked haltingly, her eyes round as quarters as she squeezed Julie's hand. Julie tried to understand how overwhelming an airport must be for Alina after seeing only the inside of an orphanage her whole life.

"Let's go get our suitcases," Julie said brightly, thinking Alina—like most kids—might enjoy watching the bags circle past. She guided her daughter toward the luggage carousel. "Do you see our bags?" she asked Mark, who was standing a few feet away.

"Not yet," he replied.

In that instant of interaction, Julie loosened her grip on Alina's hand, and Alina flew with astonishing speed onto the carousel.

"Alina!" both Julie and Mark cried.

Julie lunged forward, bumping an older woman on the shoulder, but the hem of Alina's shirt slipped through her fingers.

"Mark, get her!" Julie said.

"What does it look like I'm doing?" Mark shoved past people and bags, nearly diving onto the moving belt himself.

"Excuse me, excuse me." Julie pushed past people crowded around the carousel to get closer to Alina, but her daughter paid no attention. She continued to crawl over the suitcases, pulling at tags and handles. In another five feet, she'd slip through the rubber barrier and be on the dark other side of the carousel.

Finally, Mark caught Alina's hand and pulled her toward him. Alina shrieked as though he had broken her arm, and Julie felt herself flushing at the disapproving glares they were receiving. *I'm sorry*, she wanted to say. *This is her first day in America, her first day outside an orphanage—we're doing our best!* But Mark was carrying her away from the carousel as she thrashed, and he jerked his head toward Julie.

"The bags are right there, grab them and meet me outside," he said.

Julie nodded and excused herself another dozen times as she angled closer to the carousel.

They rushed to their SUV, where it took Mark from the outside and Julie from the inside to strap Alina into her car seat. She was red-faced and screaming, trying to throw herself in every direction, and Mark and Julie were both breathing hard when they belted themselves into their own seats. Mark looked at Julie with astonishment. Julie felt just as stunned.

"What the hell was that about back there?" he asked.

"I'm sure it's normal," Julie said, trying to reassure herself as much as Mark. "Just imagine how overwhelming all this is for her."

They spoke loudly over Alina's wailing. Mark looked at Julie skeptically. "Does this sound normal to you?"

Julie unbuckled her seatbelt. "I'm going to sit in the back and try to comfort her." She resituated herself in the back seat next to Alina. As Mark reversed, she said soothingly, "It's okay, honey. It's okay. We're going home."

With a jolt of surprise, Julie realized something strange: though Alina was throwing a tantrum for the ages, she wasn't crying. Not one tear had dried on her cheeks or shone in her eyes.

"Mark," she said quietly, as they merged onto the freeway, "have you seen her cry?"

Mark glanced at Julie in the rearview mirror. "What do you mean? She's been crying since we got to the airport."

"No," Julie said. "Screaming, yes, but not crying. No tears. She didn't cry when we left the orphanage, either. Didn't even protest a bit."

"Well, she couldn't have been too sad to leave that place."

"No, but . . . it's all she knew. You'd think . . . I don't know. It just seems strange to me that it would be that easy to leave what was home, even if it wasn't a nice one."

"We'll mention it to the pediatrician. Don't worry—I'm sure you're right, and all of this is just a phase. Now for part two of the day: introducing her to Luke. How do you think that'll play out?"

Julie looked at Alina, who had quieted and was staring out the window with that expression of frozen watchfulness. "At this point?" she said. "I have no idea."

Lucas had been staying with Julie's parents, who had arranged to be waiting at the Ryans' when they arrived. When Mark turned the corner onto their street, they saw cars clogging the driveway and lining the road in front of their house.

"Seriously?" Mark asked. "After what happened at the airport, I'm not so sure about this."

Julie quickly recognized her brothers' and sisters' cars, along with her parents' sedan and a cousin's minivan. "So typical!" she said, half-annoyed and half-pleased at the surprise welcome. "No one knows how to give anyone any privacy."

Mark pulled the car over at the curb and took a deep breath as he cut the engine. "Well, nothing we can do about it now. Here we go."

Alina let Julie unbuckle her from the car seat and carry her toward the house, though she was limp in Julie's arms. Her eyes were wide, taking in the two-story homes, the gleaming cars, the trees just starting to bud. Once again, Julie wondered what this all looked like to her. Had she seen anything beyond the pitiful gray grounds of the orphanage?

"This is home," Julie said, smiling at Alina. "Can you say *home?*"

Alina watched her closely but didn't respond.

When Mark opened the door, the house exploded with noise. Lucas had a few friends over, and they all jumped up from the couch, where they were playing Wii, and joined Julie's parents and siblings in rushing to greet them.

"Welcome home, honey!" her mother cried, kissing Julie on the cheek. She gasped, and a lock of silvery hair fell over her eye as she gazed at Alina. "And you must be Alina," she cooed, touching a hand to the child's cheek. Alina flinched, yelping and squirming in Julie's arms. "Oh, it's okay, sweetie," Julie's mother tried again. "I'm your grandma."

Alina's face was reddening, and Julie rushed to say, "She's just overwhelmed."

Lucas, who had been hanging a few feet back, looked at Alina and then up at Julie and Mark. Julie smiled reassuringly.

"You can come closer," she said softly. "Come meet your sister."

Lucas had an excited, bewildered, uncertain air to him as he stepped forward. "Alina," he said quietly, "I'm your brother. My name is Lucas."

Alina stopped squirming and watched him. The baby house only kept children up to four years old; Lucas was nine. This was probably her first interaction with an older child.

Lucas reached a hand toward her, as gently as if she were a baby animal. Alina didn't move when he touched her shoulder.

"Does she talk? Does she know any English?" he asked.

"Very little, if anything," Mark said, "and we're not sure how much of this she understands."

"Well, she should eat something," Julie's mother said briskly. "Look at her—she's so tiny!"

Julie felt unreasonably defensive. "We're taking her to the pediatrician on Monday. But for now—I smell pizza. Eat, everyone! I'm going to take your advice, Mom, and make something for Alina to eat."

Julie was exhausted but wired as she carried Alina into the kitchen. The smell of pizza grew stronger, and she saw two boxes on the stove, the lids already lifted. Alina whimpered.

"What is it, honey?" Julie asked, setting her down. "Are you hungry? Let's get you some dinner."

Julie had asked the orphanage staff what kind of food the children ate so that she could be prepared when Alina arrived at their home. She wasn't given many specifics—just told that the meals included fruit, meat, and vegetables. Since Julie wasn't sure what foods Alina was accustomed to eating, she decided to play it safe and not give her pizza. While Alina stood close by, her back to the wall, Julie steamed carrots and broccoli and quickly grilled some chicken. She cut two strips into small pieces, leaving the other two on a cutting board by the stove. Alina's whimpers were louder now, and Julie hurried to place her and the plate at the table.

As soon as she sat down, Alina grabbed the food with both hands and jumped up, running to a corner the way she had at the orphanage with the banana.

"Alina!" Julie said, startled. "Be careful, honey. That food is hot." She stepped closer to Alina to guide her back toward the table but stopped when she saw the wildness in Alina's eyes. In that moment, she reminded Julie of a cornered animal, all survival instincts. Alina never removed her gaze from Julie as she stuffed her mouth with vegetables and chicken. When she finished with the food she had grabbed, Alina ran back to the table and snatched the rest, returning to her corner to eat. Julie stared, dumbstruck. She had never seen such a thing before—such desperation. Alina whimpered constantly as if she were upset, but she just kept eating and eating. *What happened to you?*

The only word Alina spoke the rest of the night was, "Mama." Anytime Julie moved more than a few feet away, Alina cried out as if she were being abandoned. "Mama! Mama!" But when Julie tried to hold her, she stiffened and pulled away. Julie's relatives watched with a mixture of fascination, pity, and unease.

When everyone finally left, Julie, Mark, and Lucas decided to show Alina her bedroom. The walls were painted lilac, and the twin bed was covered with a purple princess comforter. There was a small nightstand with a little fairy lamp and a chest of drawers with a mirror above it. Julie had been unable to get specifics on Alina's preferences, so she'd tried to pick out a bedroom theme that Alina would find appealing.

"This is your room, sweetheart," Julie said, holding Alina's hand. She gestured to everything in the room and then back at Alina. "This is all yours now."

"Me?" Alina said, startling them all. She was frozen as she took everything in.

Mark knelt down beside her. "Yes, it's all yours."

"What was her orphanage like?" Lucas asked quietly.

Julie knew that he often took their home and the comfort of their life for granted and was proud of him for recognizing how different Alina's experience must have been. "It was pretty bleak, honey," Julie said. "She's been sleeping with twenty others to a room her whole life.

This is a huge change. Luke, why don't you say goodnight to your sister? It's time to get her ready for bed."

"Goodnight, Alina," Lucas said, almost shyly. He knelt down beside Mark but didn't try to her hug her. "See you tomorrow."

Alina looked from Lucas to Mark, then back up to Julie.

"Should I get a bath running for her?" Mark asked.

"That would be great," Julie said. "Thank you. I'll get her undressed and meet you in there."

When Mark and Lucas had left the room, Julie smiled at Alina. Exhaustion was making her head spin a little. She couldn't believe that this time yesterday, they were still in Russia.

"Okay, honey," Julie said. "We're going to take a bath now. Let's get you out of those stinky plane clothes."

Alina was wearing a fuchsia cardigan over a white Baby Gap tee and blue jeans they had brought for her to change into at the orphanage. When Julie reached to slip the cardigan off of Alina's shoulders, she backed up toward the bed and screamed, "No!" She clutched at the sweater, pulling it tightly around her diminutive frame.

"I'm not taking it away from you, honey. These clothes need to be washed, and we're just going to take a super quick bath." Julie mimed washing her hair, but Alina clearly didn't understand. It took fifteen minutes to get a yelling, hitting, and kicking Alina out of her clothes; the whole time, Julie worried that she was traumatizing her own daughter. What if Alina had been through something awful at the orphanage and this was bringing back memories? But then, she *had* to have a bath sometime soon. Plus, she needed her diaper changed, and moms always took care of that. Alina needed to understand that

Julie was her mother, that she was not going to hurt her, and that this was good for her.

After the bath—during which Alina defecated in the water once, forcing them to empty the small tub and start over—Julie carried her back to the room and changed her into a clean cloth diaper. It should have been far too small for a five-year-old, but Alina was so tiny that it fit her perfectly. It deeply worried Julie that Alina wasn't yet potty-trained; it indicated a level of neglect and lack of care that made her shudder. The doctor's appointment on Monday couldn't come soon enough.

"Why don't you try rocking her to sleep?" Mark asked quietly, standing in the doorway. "She's probably never had that before, and maybe it will help."

Julie looked up from where she sat with Alina on the floor. "Thinking that no one has ever rocked her breaks my heart," she whispered. She reached for Alina, but as usual, she stiffened up. Her limbs tightened until Julie felt she had scooped a mannequin into her lap. "Let's put you to bed now, sweetie."

Julie sat with Alina on the edge of the bed, humming and rocking her gently. Alina squirmed. Her face reddened as she tried to break free. Finally, Julie looked again at Mark. His eyes were tired behind his smudged glasses. "She doesn't like it."

Alina wriggled away and crawled to the corner of the bed against the wall. When Julie lay on her back beside her, Alina slowly did the same. Then she did something strange: she rubbed her head against the wall, mewling like a kitten as she stared straight at the ceiling.

CHAPTER 4
VOICES

"Row, row, row your boat, gently down the stream. Merrily, merrily, merrily, merrily, life is but a dream."

Life is but a dream . . . life is but a dream.

Mama singing. Alina sitting, Mama behind. Two of them in mirror, sitting, singing, staring. Fingers reaching toward eyes in mirror.

"Yes, honey, that's you."

In orphanage, mirror in crib. Tap, tap, tap. Poking eyes.

"How about we comb out your hair? Make it nice and silky?"

Mama in a red sweater, bright red! Mama opening drawer, pulling something out, and then closing the drawer. Alina wanted to see inside! Pulling drawer, yanking. Harder, harder.

"Alina, honey, you're going to pull it out of the dresser. Let go now."

Mama speaking, getting louder. Noises up and down, louder, softer. Alina couldn't understand, but she knew Mama meant *no* because she was pushing on the drawer and not letting Alina see inside. Alina pulled harder. Wood rasping wood, fingers clasped around knob.

"Alina, come on now. Stop that!"

Mama's hand on Alina's wrist.

"No!" Alina shrieked.

Mama's eyes in the mirror got big. Alina's eyes in the mirror got small.

"Mine!" Alina yelled.

Mama, quiet now. Then she sang, "Row, row, row your boat, gently down the stream . . ."

Alina stared. Heart pounding. Still pulling drawer. Mama was reaching something toward Alina's head—brown, spiky. Touching Alina's hair.

"No!" Run! Run!

Old orphanage lady, mean, with white hair: *All you kids are crawling with lice. We'll have to chop all your hair off to get rid of them. Come here, hold still.*

Metal, light bouncing. Fingers in handles, long nails. *Ckks, ckks, ckks.* Blades.

You stop moving! This is for your own good, you've got bugs all over you. If you don't stop moving, you'll make me cut you!

Ckks, ckks, ckks. Alina screaming, screaming. Hair falling. Light hair on gray floor, mixing with dark hair, red hair, curly hair, straight hair. *Ckks, ckks, ckks.* Alina kicking, thrashing. Then—

Damn, see what you made me do!

Wet on Alina's cheek. Red on her fingers, bright red! Staring. Tasting. Red on her tongue like the blades smelled to her nose—sharp.

All of you in here, you're like broken toys.

Alina with her back against the wall. Mama in her bright red sweater. Voice soft, trembly.

"It's just a comb, sweetheart. Your hair is so tangled. The comb won't hurt you, and neither will I," Mama said softly.

Alina did not believe the soft voice. Voices could be soft, loud, low, high, whisper, yell, nice, mean—voices changed, voices lied. Finally, Mama looked at Alina, put the comb down, and then they both looked in the mirror.

CHAPTER 5
HEALTHY RANGES

Caring for Alina brought with it all the challenges of caring for a young child—and then some. She didn't communicate well through language, and Julie and Mark's efforts to guess her desires often fell short, leaving them feeling confused, unsure, and inadequate. Meanwhile, Alina seemed capable of mostly three emotional expressions: neutral wariness, fear, or anger. When she was introduced to some of the neighbors over the weekend, Alina either ran clumsily to a wall she could press her back against, staring at the person, or she hid behind Julie. Anytime she didn't get what she wanted—and what *did* she want, exactly?—she screamed, kicked, and scratched, her little arms and legs flailing in a frenzied attempt to make contact with something—anything. Her diapers constantly needed to be changed, and twice, she had pulled them off at night and soiled the bed. She whimpered every time she smelled food and kept eating with the frenetic energy of someone who didn't know when she would get her next meal. And it seemed as though she *never slept*. Anytime Julie checked on her, either on the baby monitor or in her room throughout the night, Alina was lying on her back, eyes open and blankly roving across the ceiling.

By Monday, Julie felt half-drunk with fatigue and the terrifying suspicion that all their lives had changed forever—and not in the good ways she had anticipated. She had never looked more forward to taking a child to a doctor. Julie was scared. She desperately hoped a professional like Dr. Prentiss would be able to provide some context for Alina's behavior,what they were experiencing, and what it meant for their family.

The waiting room was separated into two areas—one with chairs evenly spaced and parenting and celebrity magazines stacked on glass tables between them, and one with a children's table covered with toys, including large building blocks, dolls, a toy train, books, and an old Etch-a-Sketch. Several kids played among the toys and read books while their parents waited in the seating area. Alina sat in a chair next to Julie, who plucked a book with a dog on the cover and held it out to her daughter.

"Woof, woof, barked the dog," Julie said softly, smiling. She wondered if Alina had ever seen a dog. Maybe a pet would be good for her.

Alina leveled the book with a blank gaze as Julie offered it to her. She glanced from it to Julie with seemingly no interest. The same had been true earlier in the weekend when Julie tried to interest her in a dollhouse she'd built herself prior to Alina's arrival. Alina just didn't seem to know what to do with toys, nor did she seem aware that they were a source of fun for children.

When a smiling nurse called out Alina's name, Julie stood and extended a hand to her daughter. After a moment, Alina put her tiny and slightly clammy hand in Julie's. Together, they followed the nurse down a short hallway into the examination room. The walls were painted light blue, and a wallpaper border of kittens chasing puppies divided the top half from the bottom. The nurse asked that Alina sit on the examination bed, and the white paper crinkled as Julie settled Alina over it. Alina's lips were pursed and white, her pale eyebrows drawn, so Julie sat in a chair beside her to provide comfort.

Dr. Anthony Prentiss was Lucas's pediatrician. He was in his mid-fifties with thick graying hair and a friendly smile. With two boys of his own, he'd always been a natural with Luke, and Julie trusted him as a doctor and liked him as a person. Today, Julie watched his face carefully as he took Alina's measurements and checked her vital signs. His thick, almost bushy brows drew close together over his nose, and his brown eyes were slightly squinted as he took notes.

"All children grow at different rates, of course," he said, talking to Julie while smiling at Alina, "but you can see she's significantly undersized and underweight. The typical height for a five-year-old girl is around forty inches, and Alina is only twenty-nine inches tall. Typical weight for her age tends to be around thirty-nine pounds, and she only weighs twenty-six pounds. Do you have her health records from the orphanage?"

Julie shook her head. "All they gave us was a one-page form, which didn't tell us much about her. I feel awful—I don't even have it with me. I forgot it at home."

"That's okay," Dr. Prentiss said with a smile. "Just mail a copy or fax it as soon as you can. Tell me, though— what do you know about her parents?"

Julie told Dr. Prentiss what little they knew about Alina's parents and early life. "From what we understand, it's rare to know much more than this when you adopt internationally."

"Right." Dr. Prentiss nodded. "Well, genetics aside, nutrition and environment have also played a role here. That means that with some changes, it's possible to get her into more healthy ranges. But it also begs the question of what she experienced at the orphanage and how that might affect her going forward. How has her behavior been since she has been home?"

Julie smiled ruefully, looking at Alina. Quietly, she listed Alina's unusual behavior over the past few days, ticking it off on her fingers: the wariness, anger, and fearfulness, difficulty separating, not sleeping, the extreme tantrums with hitting and kicking, and the desperate eating habits.

"Yesterday morning," Julie said, "I went to her room to get her out of bed, and she'd taken off her diaper again. She was just laying in this mess, and she never made a sound. She never cried—in fact, in the four days we've had her, I still haven't seen her cry with tears. Luke always cried when his diaper was full—and Alina is five!"

Dr. Prentiss frowned. "Is she verbal? Is she using words to communicate?"

"She knows a few words, like *yes* and *no*, and she seems to have matched *Papa* and *Mama* to Mark and me. We've never heard her speak a word of Russian, though. Isn't that unusual?"

Dr. Prentiss didn't answer directly. "As you remember with Luke," he said, taking a seat on a stool, "kids are typically pretty talkative at this age. They love asking 'why' and engaging others in conversation, and they're con-stantly making sensory observations about the world—describing how things look, feel, sound, smell, and taste, and also what they think."

Julie nodded, adding wryly, "Luke started talking at eleven months and hasn't stopped since."

"Is she using other gestures or other actions to com-municate? Showing you things or taking your hand for something she wants?" asked Dr. Prentiss.

"Not really, at least not to tell us what she wants," said Julie. "How mad she gets tells us what she doesn't like, though!"

Dr. Prentiss pulled up a screen on his computer and typed notes as he spoke to Julie. "Some of this could be a matter of adjustment. She's only been with you for a few days and has obviously experienced extreme change, moving to a new country to live with new peo-ple, so we have to take that into consideration. For now, I would just keep doing what you're doing—provide as much nurturance, certainty, and routine as you can. It's important that she start gaining weight, so I would in-crease her calories and allow her to eat more of what she wants within healthy limits. Maybe try some differ-ent foods and try to determine what meals she prefers. I would like to see her again in two weeks to see how she's doing."

Julie nodded. "Definitely. But what if . . ." She glanced at Alina, who was watching them quietly. "What if other things don't improve? With her behavior and how angry she gets at us?"

"We'll cross that bridge if we need to," Dr. Prentiss said. "She's having a lot of new experiences right now, which can be overwhelming. If the behavioral problems do persist, though, we might wonder about a possible emotional or behavioral disorder—especially with her unknown history. At that point, we could make a referral for a psychological evaluation. If she does have some type of disorder, it would be important to get some services in place as soon as possible. For now, though, let's help her adjust to America and your family."

Julie forced herself to smile. "Thank you," she said. "We'll do that."

"It may help to keep a daily log and write down what you're experiencing with her behavior," Dr. Prentiss said. "Keep track of what and when she eats, where a tantrum occurs, and what is happening in the environment preceding it. Keeping a log may help us spot patterns."

Julie looked at Alina, who met her gaze. For less than a minute this morning, Alina had allowed Julie to briefly run her fingers through her hair, and now the fine strands gleamed under the white fluorescent light. In moments like this, when her daughter seemed content, Julie could almost convince herself that her emotions were heightened, her mind overactive from stress, and that Alina was just a little behind and everything would be fine. Yet there was also a knowing pinch in her stomach, an intuitive side of her that believed this was just the beginning of a journey and struggle.

Dr. Prentiss gave Julie a reassuring smile. "Let's focus on her physical health now. Since you don't have immunization records, we'll have to re-vaccinate her today according to the U.S. schedule. That means we're due for the first courses of Hepatitis A and B, so two vaccinations."

Julie cringed. "Okay. I want to warn you, though—based on how she acted this weekend, this is probably not going to be easy."

"Shots are tough for all kids," said Dr. Prentiss, rising from his stool. "But I have a feeling this will go just fine."

CHAPTER 6
WORLD BAD

"Alina?" Mama. "Dr. Prentiss is going to give you two little shots today. These are to keep you healthy, so you can grow up to be big and strong."

Mama smiling. Hair back from face, eyes big and blue. Looking at the man in white. Doing things with his hands—holding things, looking at Alina. Coming closer. Instantly, Alina breathing harder. Wanting to leave.

"Okay, Mom, how about you sit close to Alina for this, and maybe she can squeeze your hand. This is going to hurt just a little bit, sweetie," he said, closer to Alina, "and then we'll get you a special band-aid and a dum dum sucker!"

"Mama," Alina said, edging away from the man.

"Yes, honey, I'm right here. I'll come stand right by you and you can hold my hand. It'll be over soon, and we'll go home." Mama taking Alina's hand. Mama's hand warm, fingers wrapping around Alina's. Quiet voice to the man. "Please, let's just get this over with as soon as possible."

Alina squirming. She didn't want to hold hands. Mama rubbing Alina's back. Then cool air. No diaper. Squirming, away! Away! Quick swipe, cold and wet, on her bottom.

No! Wriggling, Mama's hand pressing on back. One more hand on legs.

"Alina, you have to be still. Come on, honey, it's okay. I'm right here."

"She's moving too much."

"Just, please, let's get it over with."

No! Holding too tight! Alina hitting Mama's legs, throwing head up and down. Feet kicking. Alina's nails, Mama's skin. PULL!

"Ow!" Mama yelled.

"Here we go, Alina." Man.

Cold! Sharp! Stab! Pain! Pain!

Alina screamed, loud as she could. Voice coming up from her toes, racing through her legs, stomach, chest, and throat, noise like thunder. Wrenching away from Mama. Mama bad! Man bad! Mama let the man hurt her! Mama was not protecting her! Alina hit Mama with her fists. Screaming.

"Oh, my God." Mama, trying to wrap Alina in her arms. "Look, her nose is bleeding. Alina, calm down! Calm down!"

Man trying to touch her. Alina hitting and kicking.

"I've never seen anything quite like this before. Let me get some tissue. Do you have her?"

Alina throwing herself, wanting Mama's hands OFF!

"For now but barely!"

"Just hold her tight."

Finally breaking free. Scrambling to the floor and then the far wall. Panting, glaring. "BAD!" Alina screamed. "BAD!"

"I—I've never heard her say that before." Mama's shaky voice.

"Here's a tissue for her nose."

Mama coming closer, Alina kicking to keep her away.

Alina bad. Others bad. World bad.

CHAPTER 7
A BREAKING POINT

The next few months seemed unreal. There were times, like the first few minutes in the doctor's office, when Alina was sweet and calm. She sat between Julie and Mark on the couch and let Julie lightly run her fingers up and down the middle of her little back, feeling each tiny ridge of her spine. Her stillness and easy breathing told them it was comforting. Smiles were rare and special gifts for which Julie and Mark were starved, each one bringing hope for more and for a future unlike the present. There were more times that she didn't rush away with food, didn't pull her diaper off at night, and didn't scream and attack her parents. There were also times that she looked at Julie with something resembling, if not affection, then at least pleasant regard. There were times—a few minutes here, an hour there—that the halcyon stilled, turmoil was absent, and Julie could rest.

Then there were the other times.

Once, Luke accidentally stepped on her toe and Alina picked up the closest item—an iron statuette of a horse—and hit him in the stomach with it. The air instantly left his chest, and he gasped and fell to his knees, where

Alina managed one more blow—leaving a half-dollar sized bruise on his collarbone—before Mark scooped her up and carried her to her room. She screamed for hours, saying nothing intelligible, and threw herself against the walls, doors, and furniture any time Mark tried to leave the room. But things were no better when he was in there. Her wailing had no end. In the pauses when she sucked in air, Mark's ears rang with the shrieks he could still hear.

Another time—Julie had weeks of nightmares over this—Alina managed to open the car door while they were on the highway. The SUV flew at sixty miles an hour while the door hung wide open and Alina thrashed in her car seat. Julie was almost paralyzed with horror at the wheel.

"Alina, no!" she yelled. "Please, stop moving! Stay still!" In a panic, Julie pulled onto the shoulder of the road and slammed the car into park. Alina was still throwing herself from side to side, but the car seat held firm, giving Julie a chance to breathe for a second, her body shaking. Julie stayed with Alina in the car on the side of the road for an hour until she calmed down enough so that they could continue driving.

Then there was the issue of sleep. Alina refused to sleep—or even stay in bed—unless Julie was in the room. Her stamina was incredible. At fifteen-minute intervals, she lifted her head off her pillow to make sure Julie was still lying on the floor, covered with the cashmere throw she'd brought in from the living room. If Julie tried to sneak out, Alina screamed. Sometimes she climbed out of bed and stood in the hallway, naked and soiled, wailing as hard as she could. Everyone in the family lost sleep when Julie didn't spend the entire night with Alina.

On an incredibly rare afternoon when Alina was napping—a sleep she seemed to tumble into out of sheer exhaustion—Luke walked into Julie's room. Julie had the lights off and the covers pulled over her head as she laid alone in their bed. Mark would be home from work in an hour, and he would help her cook dinner. Right now, though, she couldn't imagine getting out of bed.

"Mom?" Luke whispered at the doorway.

"Mmm." Julie's voice was muffled, her cheek pressed against her pillow.

"Mom, I need help with my math homework."

For a moment, a sob almost cut through Julie's throat. She fought an unprecedented impulse to yell, *Just leave me alone! I am so tired! Can't you see how tired I am?* But she hadn't spent any one-on-one, quality time with Luke since Alina had come home. Unintentionally, they were confirming Luke's fear that he'd lessen in importance once his sister arrived. Julie couldn't do that to him. She loved her son very much.

"Come get in bed next to me for a few minutes," she said, pulling herself up with a light groan. She patted the space beside her, and Luke smiled broadly. Julie smiled back. A parent and child smiling. Smiling. Such a simple and beautiful thing. Smiles had become more important to her in the last several months. *Why didn't I think more about them before? Because we take smiles for granted when we have them and miss them when they're gone? Is that why?*

Luke laid down next to Julie and showed her his math homework while she kept her head on the pillow. The worksheet was a series of multiplication problems. Math was definitely not Julie's best subject in school, and she dreaded the day he presented her with homework she couldn't understand. Fortunately, today was not that day. She spent the next twenty minutes showing Luke how to multiply fractions. He cuddled close to her, their shoulders touching. He seemed to appreciate the closeness more than the help with his homework. Although he was older and seemed so much like Mark at times, Julie was reminded of how young and vulnerable her son was when she looked into his eyes.

"Has anyone ever showed you the trick with multiplying by nine?" Julie asked, grinning.

Luke shook his head, eyes brightening.

"Hold out your two hands." Once they both had their fingers spread before them, Julie said, "Let's say you're multiplying nine times three. Lower your third finger. Now look—you have two fingers on your left and seven on your right. Twenty-seven. See?"

"No way!" Luke exclaimed. "That's awesome!"

"It only works up to ten, obviously, but it's still neat, huh?"

Luke nodded, grinning. They tried it from nine times one to nine times ten, and Luke beamed at her as if she'd shared the world's best-kept secret with him.

"Thanks, Mom," Luke said when they had finished the worksheet. "That helped me a lot."

"Of course, Luke." Julie smiled, ruffling her son's hair. "And it was great spending time with you."

Luke smiled back before quietly saying, "Hey, Mom? Can I ask you something?"

"Of course."

"I don't understand Alina. Why is she like this? Why can't she just be like other kids?"

Julie sighed and snaked an arm around Luke's skinny shoulders, clad in a basketball jersey. "I know it's been hard for you," she said, "but normal is different for everyone, Luke. Dad and I still have some things to figure out to help Alina, and trust me, we will, and it will get better around here." Julie heard herself say the words and instantly wondered how sincere they sounded to Luke, much less to herself.

"I don't like having her here. She ruins everything." Luke shrugged away from Julie, his voice growing more animated. "I can't even bring my friends over because of how she freaks out. And she's all you and Dad care about anymore. I never even get to spend time with you anymore. I miss you, Mom."

Julie reached for Luke, but he pulled away. Though he was sniffing hard, trying valiantly not to cry, tears snuck from the corners of his eyes, and he wiped them away angrily.

"I want you and Dad to send her back to Russia," he said. "She doesn't belong here. She's not part of our family."

"She is part of our family," Julie said, more sharply than she intended. "We made a commitment to her, and she's not a damaged toy we can take back to the store. We need to be patient, Luke."

But as a strategy, patience was not working well with Alina. Things hit a breaking point almost six months to the day after Alina's arrival. Julie had been sitting at the backyard patio table while Alina played in the grass. Alina didn't seem to engage in pretend play, but she did have an interest in playing with dirt and bugs. She could lay on her belly on the grass for hours, at eye level with the green blades, and just stare at the scurrying small life. At first, Julie was unnerved by Alina's fascination with insects. More than once, she'd come in from the backyard with her fingers curled around a beetle or dragonfly, and the pockets of her jeans were constantly caked with dirt. But as Julie became more desperate for a break from the tantrums and the intensity of Alina's behavior, she embraced the opportunity to let her play as she wanted. Did that make her a bad mother, letting her daughter make playmates of bugs? Julie wasn't sure, but good Lord, she cherished these times of peace.

At least they were peaceful times until it was time to call Alina inside.

"Okay, Alina," Julie said, trying to keep her voice chipper even though she was inwardly wincing. "It's five o'clock. Let's go inside and make dinner now."

Alina glanced up, just barely, and then returned her gaze to the ground. She parted blades of grass and lowered her head even further.

Damn it, Julie thought. By now she knew the pattern: if she made a request and Alina ignored or glared at her, there was going to be a meltdown. If she made a request and Alina smiled, then it would be fine. Julie and Mark were noticing other patterns as well. They had noticed that more often than not, the most intense meltdowns happened when Julie or Mark asked Alina to switch from one task to another—from playing to eating; sleeping to waking; eating to showering—and not always from a preferred to non-preferred activity. She could be switching to something they thought would be enjoyable and still have a hard time.

Julie stood up, hoping it would prompt Alina to do the

same. It didn't work. "Alina," she said again. "Come on, sweetie. Let's go inside and make some dinner for Dad and Luke."

Alina glared at Julie, not moving. Julie wasn't ever sure how to best handle these situations with her daughter.

"Okay, Alina. I'm going to count to three," Julie said, feeling stupid. What did Alina know about counting? Or what reaching "three" meant? But she didn't know what else to do. "Alina, no dessert for you tonight if I reach three. Okay, here I go . . . One . . . two . . . Don't you want ice cream, Alina?"

"No," Alina said.

Julie took a deep, unsteady breath. "Three," she said. "I'm serious now. No dessert, and it's time to come in the house. Let's go, Alina."

"No!" Alina repeated, louder.

Why couldn't Mark be here? Why couldn't *he* be the one to deal with this? *He's working,* Julie told herself. *He's doing his part. Get it together. She's only five!* Julie strode to where Alina was now sitting on the ground and took Alina's thin wrist, pulling her forcefully to her feet.

"No!" Alina shrieked. With her full strength, she kicked Julie's shin, and the blow was hard enough to make Julie see black for a second. Still gripping Alina's arm, she looked down to see an angry red mark blossoming on her skin. Alina drew her leg back to kick again, but Julie reached down and scooped the little girl into her arms, where she scratched and wailed and finally bit down hard enough on Julie's arm to draw blood. By the time Julie made it inside the house with Alina struggling in her arms, she couldn't fight her own tears anymore.

"Mom?" Luke raced downstairs at the commotion,

gasping at the sight of his mother restraining his sister in her arms. "What's going on? Are you okay, Mom?"

"Call your father," Julie gasped. "Tell him to come home now!"

Julie stumbled toward Alina's room, barely managing to maintain her grasp, and shut the door before finally setting Alina down. Alina was shrieking, her face mottled and hands balled at her sides. She ran to her nightstand, yanked the lamp from the wall, and hurled it at Julie. Feeling dazed, Julie barely dodged the lamp. Then Alina pulled at her nightstand drawer until the wood splintered and kicked it until it broke. From the nightstand, she ran to the chest of drawers and jerked all the drawers open, pulling out and throwing all the contents—underwear, pajamas, sweaters—at Julie, screaming all the while.

"Mom, Dad's on his way!" Luke called through the door. "Are you okay?"

"I'm fine," Julie managed, but she wasn't feeling fine at all. She had never felt more powerless and desperate in her life. "Alina, please try to calm down," she said, but then Alina charged right at her, knocking Julie's air out of her lungs as she stumbled off balance into the wall.

"Mom?" Luke's voice sounded fearful now.

"Go to your room, Luke!" Julie shouted.

Alina kicked and screamed and bit Julie until finally, after more struggle, Julie managed to untangle herself from her daughter's grip and slip outside the room, slamming the door shut behind her. She and Alina played tug-of-war with the door, with Alina pulling on the knob to open it and Julie also pulling on the knob to keep it closed. That was how Mark found her ten minutes later.

"What the hell is going on?" he asked, rushing toward her. "What's happening?"

Julie wept inconsolably, hiccupping through her words. "She's just going crazy. She won't stop!"

"Let me handle this now." Mark edged Julie out of the way to hold the doorknob and was able to keep it more secure while Alina pulled on the other side. Mark put his other hand to Julie's face, saw her sweat-soaked hairline and the dried blood and marks on her arms and legs. "My God," he said. His eyes were stunned. "Julie, we need help . . . I think we need to call the police."

Julie sank to the floor and sobbed with her head between her knees. Alina was still shrieking in her room, and Mark said, "You make the phone call. I'm going to try to calm her down. She's got to be hurting herself in there."

"Be careful," Julie said. She couldn't believe she was warning her six-foot-tall, hundred-and-ninety pound husband to protect himself against such a miniature child, but when Alina was like this—Julie shuddered. It was as if she were possessed.

A police car and an ambulance arrived fifteen minutes later, sirens screaming, and Julie let them into her house feeling shell-shocked. Luke watched the commotion from the upstairs landing, his face pale and worried as the EMTs wheeled a stretcher into the front hallway.

"Mom? Is someone hurt?" he asked.

"No, honey," Julie said, gesturing the EMTs forward. "Everything's going to be okay."

The police and medical technicians needed no more guidance than Alina's screams and the lower timber of Mark's voice, trying to calm Alina down. Julie could do nothing but stand in back of her husband and call out to

Alina, "Just do what they say, honey. Come on, it's going to be okay. It'll be okay" as the EMTs entered the room and tried to restrain her. Mark looked helpless as Alina pulled her usual maneuver, throwing her body from side to side as the policeman and EMTs tried to carry her over to the stretcher. She screeched and spit as they lay her down, struggling to belt her in place, and then she turned eyes of sheer terror to Julie.

"Mama, no!" she yelled. "Mama, help!"

"I'm right here, baby. I'm so sorry," Julie said, shaking and crying. "We're going, too. We'll be right behind you, okay?"

"Mama! Mama!" Alina kept screaming for Julie as the EMTs wheeled her through the house and out the front door, loading her into the ambulance.

"We'll meet you at the hospital," Mark told them.

"Please," Julie said, "turn the sirens off. She's scared. Maybe it will help her calm down. Please?"

The driver gave her a sympathetic nod as he turned off the siren noise, and the neighborhood was pitched into deep silence. Julie noticed more than one window shade moving, and she thought fiercely, *Mind your own business*.

"I'll call my mom to come watch Luke," Mark said. "Why don't you go tell him what's happening."

Julie nodded and went to tell Luke they were going with Alina to the hospital. Luke said nothing and didn't respond when she said, "See you later tonight. We love you."

Following emergency detention procedures, Alina was first taken by ambulance to the hospital emergency room for medical clearance and would then be transported to the psychiatric hospital. When they arrived at the emergency room, Alina was taken into a separate room while Mark talked to the police. They told him that Alina was "combative" when they tried to release her and that she would be restrained in the stretcher until she was emotionally and behaviorally more calm.

"Restrained?" Julie all but yelled. "Mark, she's only a child. She's probably terrified! How could you let them do that? Where is she? I need to see her."

Julie took one stride toward the reception area, which was bustling behind a glass partition, before Mark took her elbow and pulled her back. Tensely, he said, "Did you already forget why we're here? We couldn't control her, and now the police have stepped in. That's the way it works. We can't see her now. She'll start screaming the minute you walk into the room. Just let these people do their jobs."

Julie glared at him, fighting the words bubbling into her throat, but she swallowed them back. "All right. Fine. What are we supposed to be doing, though? Who do we talk to around here?"

Mark waved a clipboard. "They gave this to me to fill out. The sooner we're done, the sooner we'll know what's going to happen."

Mark and Julie sat on maroon chairs in the waiting area, beyond which was a hallway where doctors and nurses walked past. Some exchanged brisk or laughing greetings, and others marched quietly on. Julie wanted to yell at the ones who were chatting and laughing. Didn't they realize what has happening to her daughter and family? Why couldn't they show more respect? It seemed to her as brashly irreverent as telling dirty jokes at a funeral.

Mark filled out the paperwork while Julie sat and tried unsuccessfully to calm her nerves. Eventually, once Alina calmed, she was released from the stretcher and checked over by a doctor. With medical clearance, the police were authorized to transport her to a psychiatric inpatient hospital for a maximum seventy-two-hour evaluation. This time, Alina was taken via police car. Though she was still upset, yelling and letting no one touch her, she was no longer out of control.

At the psychiatric hospital, Alina was taken into an examination room by one of the hospital staff, a nice young man named Henry. Julie and Mark sat in the waiting room. Mark's eyelids were puffy, his striped work shirt wrinkled. Julie ran a hand through her curly hair. She didn't think she'd looked in a mirror in days. It seemed there were no words between them.

Half an hour after they arrived, a clinical social worker brought them coffee in Styrofoam cups. Nancy was a pleasantly round woman with a gemstone cross pendant grazing her collared shirt.

"I thought you could use this," she said, smiling gently. "I'm Nancy. I'll take you to see Dr. Jenkins, one of the child and adolescent psychiatrists here."

"Thank you," Julie said, rising unsteadily. She held the coffee tightly, comforted by the warmth, but didn't dare lift it to her lips until they were sitting in Dr. Jenkins's office; she didn't trust herself not to spill it if she tried to sip and walk at the same time.

"Just take a seat here for a minute," Nancy said. Her pendant glinted in the overhead light. "Dr. Jenkins will be right with you. Can I get you anything else while you wait?"

Julie and Mark shook their heads numbly, and Nancy smiled again as she left the room.

When Julie and Mark were almost done with their coffee, the door opened, and Dr. Jenkins shook their hands. He was tall, with a perfectly oval head and a pale mark on his finger suggesting a longtime wedding ring had recently been removed.

"Alina is calmer now and seems to be doing better at this point than when she arrived," he said, circling the room to occupy his desk. "I want to assure you both that your daughter will be well taken care of here. Now, if you don't mind, I'd like to get some information about Alina."

For the next twenty minutes, Dr. Jenkins asked questions about Alina, including her history and current presentation and behavior, and what had led up to her parents calling the police.

"After considering everything you've both told me and also meeting with your daughter," Dr. Jenkins said, "I would like to admit Alina to the hospital for an evaluation."

Mark deliberately did not look at his wife, anticipating her instinctive refusal. "What kind of evaluation?" he asked. "For how long?"

"Less than three days or seventy-two hours total, which is the maximum time allowed without court proceedings," Dr. Jenkins said. "During her time here, we would ensure that she stabilizes emotionally and behaviorally and does not present a danger to herself or others. I would also like to examine and try some options with medication, as she has been having some persistent difficulties, especially in regulating her emotions. Psychotropic medication can be quite helpful. At the end of her stay here, we will give you some after-care recommendations on additional therapy resources and what we think would be helpful going forward."

Julie's eyes stung with tears. "Medication, though? Doctor, she's only five years old."

"I know, and this is a struggle for parents. The hope is that with the right kind of therapy and supports, there will be improvement that makes the medication less necessary over time. The issue right now is that your daughter is at a point where the brain-based internal controls for modulating emotion are often compromised, which results in her becoming quite easily overwhelmed and having difficulty returning to a rational state. With this being the case, a psychopharmacological intervention, such as an initial course of psychotropic medication would be warranted."

Julie's head buzzed with the words Dr. Jenkins was using: *brain-based controls . . . compromised . . . psychopharmacological intervention*. Never, in all the time they had anticipated Alina's homecoming, had this scene entered her mind. She felt hopeless and depleted.

"I'll know more about any recommendations after I have more time to interview your daughter, review all the records, and talk with the staff that will be working with her at the hospital. Right now," Dr. Jenkins said, preemptively rising from his chair, "if you don't have any more questions, I'll have Nancy go through some more paperwork with you. Thanks, folks, and we'll talk soon."

With a nod and a round of quick handshakes, Dr. Jenkins was out the door. Julie took a long, slow breath. "I feel horrible leaving her here. But—"

"I think we have to, Julie," Mark interrupted. "This is for the best."

"If you'd given me half a chance to finish, I would have said the same thing," Julie said crisply, instantly regretting how snappy she sounded.

They sat in silence until Nancy returned to guide them through the forms, reassuring them again that Alina would be fine, that they could call and talk to a nurse whenever they wanted, and that they could arrange for a visit the following day.

As they left the hospital and walked to the car, Julie's chest felt as though it were splitting wide open, like a tree being separated by an axe. Bizarrely, perhaps, she missed her daughter so much it hurt.

CHAPTER 8
OKAY

Quiet. Alone. In a room that was different from the room at home. Bed at home, purple sheets. Orange lamplight. Mama usually wrapped in a blanket on the floor. Alina looking at her, scared she would go away, but Mama there. Mostly. Now alone. No Mama. White room, with white sheets that were hard to pull back. A window, glass. Alina sliding her hands, pulling and grunting. The glass would not move.

Walking around the room. Sitting, standing, walking again. Climbing up close to the window and pounding. Sitting, with back to wall. Watching the door and listening. People were passing by. Could hear footsteps and voices. Waiting.

Inside, Alina felt frozen. Remembering screaming at Mama and Papa, hitting and kicking. Bad. Alina feeling bad. Stomach knotted and feeling empty. Head hurting now. Sorry. Very sorry. It was so hard to stop getting upset.

Orphanage lady. *You'd better be a good girl or your American mommy and daddy won't want you anymore. Don't ever forget that. They return bad boys and girls. Just stick 'em on a plane, and then they're back here, with us. Back with me. You'd better be a good girl or else. Do you understand?*

Mama. *We'll be back for you soon. I promise.*

But Mama was gone and Papa was gone. Not coming back? Alina was bad. World—spinning, unsteady, dangerous, scary. New orphanage, here?

You'd better be a good girl or else.

She remembered earlier—lying in bed, couldn't move, arms being held to sides. Yelling, kicking, holding tight to the sheets. Her head filled with red and black. A feeling like falling. Screaming for Mama, Mama, help! Mama was not coming.

You'd better be a good girl or else.

Alina needed to be good or else.

The door opened. A woman walked in. "Hi, Alina."

Alina staring. Stranger.

"My name is Nancy. I just wanted to stop in and see how you're doing. Maybe let you know how things work around here." Woman smiling. Big forehead, shiny lips. "So, how are you feeling today?"

Feeling. Alina crossing arms, staring.

"Alina, do you have any idea why you're here?"

No.

"I know this is all new. Your parents love you very much, and they want to make sure you're feeling safe. It sounds like it was hard at home today, right?"

Staring.

"You're going to stay with us for a little while—maybe a few days. We're going to help you feel better. What do you think of that?"

Staring. Hearing words like *parents, love, safe.*

"How about we draw some pictures? Here, I brought

some paper and crayons." Woman smiled, putting them on the desk next to the bed.

"How about coming over here and drawing with me for a few minutes?"

Alina didn't move. Saying nothing.

Woman still smiling but looking at her watch. "Alina, do you understand what I'm asking?"

Alina could tell. The woman smiled but was not happy. Lying with her voice.

"Okay. I'll come back and talk to you later. Some of our other staff here will be stopping in soon to see how you are doing and show you the group area."

Woman walking out. Door closed again. Room quiet.

Later, same woman and a different man. "Alina, I'm Dr. Jenkins. We're going to give you some medication now. Open your mouth. Ahhh." Man's mouth a skinny O. Pink tongue. Funny looking.

Alina smiled.

"Come on now. Open up, like this, and let Nancy put the medicine under your tongue."

Another skinny O. The man pointing at Alina and then at his mouth. Alina opened hers.

"That's a good girl. Thank you."

Woman putting something white and chalky in Alina's mouth. Bitter, mouth watering.

"No, keep your mouth shut. Go on. Here's some water."

Alina grabbed the water, backing up toward wall, glaring at both of them.

"That's very good, Alina."

Later, the new orphanage lady walking with Alina to a big room. It had a TV like at Mama and Papa's house. Chairs, books, and games.

"How are you doing now, Alina?"

Alina spotted a book, a shiny cover. Grabbing it.

"Are you feeling okay? Anything you want to talk about?"

Okay. Alina remembered Mama saying, "It's okay, honey. It's all going to be okay."

"Okay," Alina said. It was a new word for her. A little louder. "Okay."

Now the woman was smiling big. "Very good."

CHAPTER 9
BEST BEHAVIOR

Julie and Mark visited Alina the day after she was admitted to the hospital. They weren't sure what to expect—would she be fine, or would she rage? Maybe even cry, finally, after she saw them? But in a small common area, Alina sat quietly with her hands in her lap, staring at them with her watchful eyes and occasionally offering the gift of a corner of her mouth lifting in a smile. She seemed . . . placid. Tired. Content and pleased to see her parents, yet more disconnected.

On the third day, the Ryans met with Dr. Jenkins and Nancy. "Alina has been here for a few days now," Dr. Jenkins said. "She's done well, has been emotionally and behaviorally stable since her admission, and does not appear to be at risk for harming herself or others. As you know, we also started her on Abilify, which is a medication that is prescribed for severe, potentially harmful behaviors caused by psychiatric problems. It has been difficult to communicate with her, as she has not responded to any communication with us. Her use of English is obviously limited, but we also haven't been able to engage in any back-and-forth activities, even play and drawing. She seems to have a tendency to shut down when people request interaction." Dr. Jenkins paused, dark eyes flicking between Julie and Mark. "Is what I'm describing typical of what you see at home?"

"You mean when she's not screaming like a maniac?" Mark regretted his harsh words instantly, but the stress was getting to him. He hadn't slept in what felt like weeks, and his performance at work was suffering. Late at night, he fantasized about leaving. Buying some used camper van, ditching his cell phone, and driving cross country, wherever he chose, free of the burdens he now carried. The fantasy brought with it equal parts guilt and resentment, so that sometimes he held Julie tenderly and other times, he pushed her away. He felt on the brink of insanity.

Julie shook her head in silent reproach. "She's gotten better than when she first arrived," she told Dr. Jenkins. "She uses some words, but she's certainly not conversational with us in a meaningful way. Can you tell us why that is?"

"Our job is to make sure your daughter is stable, and we've done that," Dr. Jenkins said. "Going forward, though, the picture is quite complex given Alina's history, current presentation, and apparent developmental delays, including communication and language problems. I understand that you've been trying to help her adjust to America and your home over the past six months—I'm interested in your thoughts on her going to school?"

School. Julie shook her head. It seemed so far away for Alina. Luke had started first grade when he was five, the same age as Alina. Still, she couldn't imagine Alina in any kind of traditional public school classroom. Would she ever get to a point where she could drop her daughter and son off at school in the morning, and Alina would sit at a desk, listen to the teacher, complete her work, and not disrupt and create chaos in the room? Julie and Mark had hoped that Julie's decision to stay home for six months would be helpful. They hoped this mother-daughter time would help Alina's adjustment to her new family and prepare her for school. But instead, they were now sitting in a psychiatric hospital.

"We aren't sure what to do about school right now, Dr. Jenkins," said Julie, and Mark nodded.

"Well, I've been doing this for quite a long time now, and I've worked a bit with the schools. When you enroll your daughter in public school, I strongly encourage you to consider a referral for an IEP evaluation—IEP means individualized education program. You would talk to the school principal or administrator about the referral. The team would then evaluate your daughter for special education and see if she requires any additional services or support in school. There are a number of variables in your daughter's situation, and school is a big piece. I also think that given Alina's behavior and the delays, it is reasonable to expect that she may require special education, so a referral is warranted. I would be concerned about her being in a traditional kindergarten in public school at this point."

"That's very helpful," Julie said, though she felt entirely overwhelmed.

"What about the rages, though?" Mark asked. "That's what brought us here in the first place, Doctor. It seems as though everything is a trigger and nothing—I mean *nothing*—seems to calm her down."

"Alina did not have any rages or meltdowns here, Mr. Ryan, but I wouldn't say that is unusual. The hospital is a different kind setting, so novel, and not many explicit expectations are placed upon patients. The goal, obviously, is short-term emotional stability." Dr. Jenkins paused to look at a folder on his desk. "The notes say that Alina preferred to spend time in her room, though she did go to a group session with some coaxing from our psychologist."

"And how did that go?" Julie asked.

"She sat with three other patients and seemed to be in a good mood, but she was either unwilling or unable to meaningfully participate."

"So you're saying she didn't have any rages at all?" Mark asked, almost aggressively, as if Dr. Jenkins hadn't spoken. "She didn't have any kind of tantrum here?"

"I know it might sound hard to believe, sir, but that is what I'm telling you." Dr. Jenkins handed Mark and Julie each a copy of a report. "At this point, it may be helpful to go over Alina's aftercare plan, which is a summary of our recommendations. First, we recommend you connect with the local public school about an IEP team referral for special education so that services can start fairly soon after she starts school if they are necessary. Second, we recommend that your daughter continue to receive the prescribed medication."

For a moment, Julie and Mark just stared at each other. The road before them seemed to stretch ever further, curving endlessly around corners they could not yet see.

"Medication," Julie said softly. "I was hoping that would be short-term, just to calm her down. Are you sure that's the right away to go? She's so young, and we don't know what she's been through. Maybe she experienced some trauma. I just don't know if medication will help if the problems aren't . . . I don't know, *biochemical*."

"I'm going to be honest," said Dr. Jenkins, leaning forward. "Yes, we are learning more about the use of medication with children, and sometimes it isn't helpful, but given Alina's behavior right now, I believe this is a good course of action. It may prove to be a necessary part of her treatment. We'll know more once we see how she responds."

"But treatment of *what*?" Mark cut in. "What is going on with her? What's making her act like this? And outside of medicating her, which we obviously don't want to do, how can we help her?"

"We know your daughter struggles with emotional regulation—or becomes easily frustrated and irrational, and has great difficulty calming," Dr. Jenkins said patiently. "As I said, the medicine should be helpful for those symptoms. Given the severity of Alina's behavior right now and the impact on the family, I think it would be helpful to contact your county department of human services. They should be able to tell you about resources such as parent support groups, respite services, and crisis intervention services so that if this happens again, the police would not have to be contacted."

If this happens again. Julie worked hard to keep herself calm, letting her hands rest lightly on the thin mahogany arms of the chair, rather than white-knuckle it the way she wanted to. *Listen to him*, she ordered herself. She reached for her purse and ignored Mark's annoyed glance as she fumbled inside for a pen. As Dr. Jenkins continued talking, she jotted down notes on the back of Alina's aftercare plan. At this point, she didn't care if they were already written; she just needed to be doing something.

"We are also recommending that you arrange for the services of an outside therapist to meet with Alina and with both of you to learn more behavior management strategies to be used in the home. Last, given your daughter's history and presentation, while it is good to have a special education evaluation, I am also recommending a comprehensive psychological evaluation by a licensed clinical child psychologist. We can provide you with a few names. You should also check with your insurance company about in-network coverage."

Psychiatrists, therapists, psychologists, insurance, in-network coverage . . . what exactly is the coverage in our plan? Mark knew that deductibles and out of pocket expenses in his work plan kept rising and that they were going up again next year. *We just see medical doctors now, and those bills are tough to pay—how are we going to manage this? What can I do?*

Dr. Jenkins continued, "Alina's case is complex, and there are a number of questions about development, learning, and areas such as adaptive, social, and behavioral functioning. The primary reasons for the psychological evaluation is to get answers to these questions, help with diagnostic impressions, and therapeutic recommendations. You will also see on the aftercare plan that the discharge diagnoses at this time, given her short stay here, are Mood Disorder – Not Otherwise Specified and Oppositional Defiant Disorder. The more formal psychological evaluation should be helpful going forward."

Julie was on overload now. *Mood disorder something specified, defiance disorder?* She scribbled wildly as her heart pounded. This was her little girl he was talking about!

"I want to take her home right now," Julie blurted.

Both Mark and Dr. Jenkins looked at her, and even as her words settled in the room, she knew they weren't completely true. The three days Alina had been at the hospital had been a bittersweet reprieve. Julie had slept in her own bed, scooped into the curve of Mark's body, and in the morning, they and Luke enjoyed breakfast the way they used to. The rushed commands Julie had once considered stressful—"Hurry up and finish your breakfast! Did you put your homework in your backpack? Luke, go brush your teeth, do you think I can't tell?"—now felt sweetly scripted, like an old sitcom in which they had all tacitly agreed to return to former roles. In the evenings, Julie and Mark sat on the couch with Luke between them, watching what he wanted until nine, when they tucked him in and returned to the living room with glasses of wine. *Is this what life was like before?* Julie had asked one night, legs tucked beneath her. She started to cry. *Did we appreciate it then, do you think? Will we ever have it again?* That night, Mark had set his glass down and cupped both her cheeks in his hands, wiping her tears with his thumbs. He didn't say anything.

"Here is Alina's prescription. You can have it filled at our pharmacy if that would be helpful." Dr. Jenkins ripped two sheets off the small pad and passed them to Julie, who slipped them into her purse. She'd add it to the binder she'd begun to assemble for Alina's documents. Like a perverse version of a baby album, it contained daily typed logs of Alina's behavior, as Dr. Prentiss had suggested, and also dates and reasons for doctors' appointments. Now she would have to add a section called "Hospitalizations." *Way to stay on top of it, Mom,* she thought angrily.

"Can you take us to Alina now? We want to see her," Mark said.

Dr. Jenkins walked them down a hallway. The walls were white, and the doors they passed were wood with metal handles. With a key card, he opened the door to Alina's room.

The room was clean and quiet—almost stark— just as it had been when they'd left her there. Alina sat at the edge of the bed, staring intently at her fingers. When the door opened, she looked up and her eyes flashed with recognition. She hopped to her feet, a look of guarded happiness on her face.

"Alina," Julie said, smiling.

"Mama," Alina replied. "Papa."

"How are you doing, honey?"

"Okay," Alina said.

Julie broke into a smile. "Did you hear that, Mark?" she asked softly.

Mark smiled back, but the expression didn't reach his eyes. "That's good, Alina. We're here to take you home now."

"Home," Alina repeated, but she didn't move from her spot by the bed until Julie came closer, putting a light hand to her shoulder. Then, looking straight ahead, Alina followed them out the door.

CHAPTER 10
ASSESSMENTS

Two weeks later, Mark and Julie met with Dr. Sheila Brook while an office worker watched over Alina in the waiting room. Dr. Brook was a clinical child psychologist in her early sixties, dressed in dark slacks and a printed blouse. She was one of those women, Julie observed, who made white hair look attractive, and her office was small and soothing, with walls painted a calm light blue and white bookshelves encompassing one wall. The couch on which they sat was cream-colored leather, and Julie wondered how Dr. Brook kept it clean with all the children she had in her office. Already, Julie imagined Alina taking a Sharpie or a pair of scissors to it.

"So how has Alina been since you brought her home from the hospital?" Dr. Brook asked.

Julie sighed. "She was quiet and pretty docile for the first day, maybe two," she said. "But then it was as if she'd been bottling up all her anger and anxiety and fear. The first time I tried to leave her in her room at night, she was raging again. It went on for a long time." Julie leaned forward, praying Dr. Brook would know what was causing this turmoil in her daughter. "What are we supposed to do? I can't sleep in her room every night. I can't spend every waking minute with her. I have another child! I have a job. I have—"

Mark put his arm around Julie, lightly squeezing the back of her neck in the soothing way she liked. She took a long, unsteady breath.

"We talked on the phone about a psychological evaluation," Dr. Brook said. "After hearing more about her history, the hospital reports, and the behavioral forms you filled out prior to this meeting, I'd like to evaluate Alina for a possible attachment disorder. Can I ask, what is your understanding of children and attachment?"

Julie perked up, like a student who knew the right answer in class. "One of our neighbors works for an employee assistance program, and he brought it up last week, so I did some reading online."

"Julie's put together a lot of information about all of this," Mark added.

Julie nodded, pulling her "Alina binder" from her briefcase. "From what I've read, attachment is the emotional bond that forms between a child—an infant—and the primary caregiver," Julie said, "and children are negatively impacted when the natural attachment process is disrupted."

Dr. Brook nodded. "Yes, babies are extremely sensitive to the interaction they receive from the primary caregiver—meaning responsiveness to their cries, regular feeding and touch, love and nurturance, all the things you remember doing, mostly naturally, with your first child. If this attachment and bonding doesn't form well, it affects a lot of areas, including a child's ability to regulate emotions, self-soothe, trust others and the world, and understand themselves. What do we specifically know about Alina's history before she was adopted?"

"We don't know much at all," Mark said. "We brought the profile the adoption agency gave us, but as far as what she experienced in the orphanage, we have no idea."

Dr. Brook nodded, taking the profile from Mark. "That's not surprising," she said. "I've heard that before from other parents. Many children adopted from foreign countries are doing quite well. Some aren't."

"This evaluation you're going to do," Mark said, "what's involved?"

"I'm going to complete a fairly comprehensive psychological evaluation designed to give us the best picture of how your daughter is doing at this time. It will be a combination of record and history review, direct testing with Alina, some home-based observation, interviews, and parent completion of some behavioral checklists—similar to the ones you completed prior to this session," Dr. Brook said. "The evaluation will include a measure of intellectual functioning, which—"

"Intellectual functioning? Do you mean her IQ?" Julie interrupted. "But she's barely verbal and certainly can't read. Aren't IQ tests done on paper, usually for older kids?"

"Actually, traditional IQ tests, or measures of intellectual or cognitive functioning, aren't all paper and pencil tests and can be used across wide age ranges," Dr. Brook explained. "These tests are often divided into two parts—generally into verbal conceptual ability and perceptual reasoning ability. However, for children with lower verbal ability or those with expressive language issues or cultural language considerations, like Alina, we are able to administer nonverbal measures of intellectual functioning."

"Okay," Mark said, though, like Julie, he was skeptical that this test would be able to accurately capture Alina's intellectual functioning. "You mentioned there are other parts to the evaluation."

"There will be some other additional direct testing that I will try with Alina, but given her language issues and level of cooperation and engagement . . ." Dr. Brook trailed off, then offered the Ryans a smile. "Well, I'll do my best. I will also want to assess Alina's level of adaptive behavior development. By that, I mean overall adaptive behavior, as well as how it breaks down into communication, daily living, and socialization skills. I'll also assess Alina's social emotional functioning through behavior ratings, interviews with you both, and observation, mostly in your home.

Julie cast Mark a mortified stare. *Home observation?* She instantly imagined all the ways it could go wrong, all the ways Alina would create a scene, and all the ways they would look like miserable failures as parents.

Dr. Brook seemed to sense their unease. "Don't worry," she said. "It's just two forty-minute blocks of time, and you don't have to do anything special to prepare. My goal is to be a fly on the wall as much as possible and just see what's happening and how she interacts—that kind of thing."

"Okay . . ." Julie said weakly.

"I'll work with you to set up dates that are convenient. In the meantime, I'd like for you to fill out some more forms for me." She opened a folder and pulled out several sheets of paper, handing them to Mark and Julie.

"I'd like you each to fill out one of these questionnaires so I can have both of your perspectives. I believe that parents are always the experts on their kids—nobody knows Alina better than you."

"Yeah, we're certainly a couple of experts, aren't we, Julie?" Mark smirked and then started to laugh.

Julie gave him a look and he immediately sobered.

"Seriously," Dr. Brook said, looking more intense but smiling warmly, "it might not seem that way, but parents are the eyes and ears of what their children say and do—so, yes, they are the experts, despite how difficult it can be to figure things out at times."

Julie smiled at Dr. Brook. She appreciated the fact that the doctor was inviting them into the process of assembling this puzzle, rather than locking them out of the room.

Together, Julie and Mark looked at the questionnaire. There were thirty statements to rate, and each parent filled one out separately. The items that both thought strongly described Alina included statements about Alina becoming stiff when hugged and upset if things didn't go her way, having poor safety awareness, breaking things, not seeming to feel guilt, not learning from consequences, having unusual eating habits and intense temper tantrums, and living in an orphanage for at least the first two years of her life.

Dr. Brook was quiet as they diligently rated each statement, and she slipped on a pair of reading glasses to review the forms when they finished. Julie didn't realize how rapidly she was tapping her foot against the rug until Mark put a hand on her knee to stop it. But she couldn't stop for long. She was as anxious and fearful as though she were waiting on the results of some biopsy.

"Your insurance will cover six hours of testing and report writing. That's not sufficient given your daughter's needs and what I would like to do—but we'll make it work," Dr. Brook said. "I also agree with Dr. Jenkins that you should request an IEP team evaluation from the school district as soon as she is enrolled, which should be soon. When my evaluation is completed, it can be added to the data used to determine whether your daughter has special education needs. You might want to wait for the results of my evaluation, but you don't need to wait for a team evaluation, no matter what you might hear from others. Now—when can you bring Alina back for our first session together?"

Julie didn't hesitate. "Your earliest availability."

CHAPTER 11
HOME VISIT

The doorbell was ringing. Ding dong! Ding dong!

"I'll get it!" Luke.

Alina twisting and turning on the couch, her eyes on door. Luke and Mama and Papa in hallway. Door opening.

"Dr. Brook, come in." Mama's cheerful voice. "Can I get you something to drink? Water, coffee?"

"I'm fine, thank you." Woman, white hair. From the other day. First, Alina thought of the mean orphanage lady. Not her. Still. Alina burrowing into couch, pulling up the blanket.

In the kitchen, some voices:

"So . . . what exactly would you like us to do?" Mama.

"Do as you normally do and forget that I'm here." Woman. "That's it."

Under blanket. More whispers from the kitchen, then footsteps. Heels on wood.

"Alina, honey?" Mama. "Remember Dr. Brook? She came by to say hi. Alina? Where is she?"

"Under the blanket." Luke. "She's so tiny, it's like she's not even there."

Cool air from blanket lifting. Mama's face close to

Alina's. Smiling. "There you are. Why don't you come on out of there and say hi to Dr. Brook?"

Alina peeking at Dr. Brook. Word, quiet: "Why?"

"Hi, Alina." Dr. Brook. "I'm just here to see your house today."

Time passing. Mama and Papa standing there. Dr. Brook sitting on a chair.

"Is this a valuable use of time?" Papa. "Our insurance is only paying for six hours, she said? If we're just going to sit here—"

"Mark."

"What?"

Silence.

"What would you normally be doing right now?" Dr. Brook.

"I—making dinner, I suppose." Mama.

"Go ahead and go about your evening as if I'm not here."

Soon—food! Smells! Alina pushing blanket away and running to kitchen. Smiling, standing barefoot by oven.

"It's hot, honey. Back up a little. Scoot back."

Alina not moving.

"Alina." Papa. "Come on. You heard your mom."

Papa's hands on her shoulders. Quick! Alina slapping Papa's hands, backing up. "Stop!" Yelling.

"Oh, God." Mama. "Damn it, Mark!"

"What do you want me to do? She's going to rush to the oven as soon as it opens and burn the skin off her hands. She's tried before!"

Alina breathing hard. Mama standing with red glove over one hand, Papa rubbing his head. Dr. Brook watching.

At the end of the second time, Dr. Brook started to talk more. She wanted Alina to draw some pictures. Blank sheets of paper, white, big. Alina ran her hands over the paper. It was smooth.

"Alina." Dr. Brook. "Let me see. Could you draw a picture of a house . . . any kind of house you'd like."

Alina holding a pencil. Staring at Dr. Brook. "House," she repeated.

"Whatever kind of house you want."

Orphanage lady. *Your new mama and papa are going to take you to a nice big house in America.*

Alina drew. Crayon moving over the page, up-down-sideways. Done.

Dr. Brook smiling. "Now draw a picture of a tree . . . any kind of tree you'd like."

Alina said "tree" and gripped the pencil. Drew a straight line with some wiggles at the top. Done.

"Okay, Alina, now draw a picture of a person . . . any kind of person you'd like." Pointing at herself, at Alina, at Mama in the kitchen. "Person."

Alina drew quickly, a circle at the top with some body parts, legs and arms. She sat on the couch, leaning over the coffee table. Done.

"Thank you, Alina. Now I'd like you to draw a picture of your family doing something."

Family. Alina looked at Dr. Brook. Stared. Put the pencil down. Looked away. Done.

CHAPTER 12
DIAGNOSIS

About a month after their first visit with Dr. Brook, Julie and Mark returned to her office hoping for answers that would point them in the right direction. Julie's mother was at home with Luke and Alina, and Julie clutched her cell phone, expecting it to vibrate at any moment with news of some crisis.

"Did you get anything from those home visits?" Mark asked. "They seemed pretty uneventful."

"Alina said something about drawing," Julie reminded him. "That was something."

Dr. Brook smiled. "Believe it or not, the entire evaluation told me quite a bit," she said. "In the first visit, I wanted to see interaction patterns in the home. That was why I asked you to do what you would normally do. That's more helpful to me than any kind of contrived situation, even if it seems uneventful. The second visit was about a little more guided interaction. That's why certain types of play were arranged."

Dr. Brook explained that she followed Dr. Stanley Greenspan's social emotional development model of relating, communicating, and thinking. Through the observations, she was trying to assess developmental capacities for shared attention and regulation, back and forth communication, engagement with others, and more complex problem solving.

"And?" Mark asked. "What did you find?"

Compared to typically developing kids her age, Alina struggles in shared attention and regulation, engagement with others, and problem solving. She becomes easily overwhelmed and frustrated, emotionally escalates rapidly, has difficulty self-soothing, and is not responsive to attempts by others to assist her in returning to a calm state. Back and forth communication, even reciprocity with gestures, is difficult for her. Play with others is not interactive and not parallel, either. Her play is restricted as far as interests and fairly isolated in nature. Toys and dolls, things like that, are new to her, and she's not quite sure how to make sense out of them."

"Right," Julie agreed, knowing exactly the blank, disinterested stare Dr. Brook had probably seen. "To her, a toy and a rock may as well be the same thing. What does all this mean, though?"

"Alina has underdeveloped social emotional skills that are necessary for age-appropriate relating, communicating, and thinking," Dr. Brook said matter-of-factly. "She needs help to boost up these basic capacities."

"What about the pictures?" Mark asked, skepticism in his voice. "Did those tell you anything?"

Dr. Brook acknowledged his tone with a motherly smile. "I know it seems like a stretch," she said, "but you can tell a lot about a child by where they go with their drawings. Kids don't verbally communicate as well as adults, so any drawings and play are a window to their internal experiences. Her response to the family drawing, for example, is noteworthy."

"How so?" asked Mark.

"While Alina at least attempted the other drawings, she did not draw anything for the family drawing. She refused. Or she wasn't sure what to draw. Either way, it means something, and I am leaning toward Alina not quite understanding yet what *family* means."

Julie felt a stab of hurt. "But we've completely embraced her into our lives as our daughter and Luke's sister," she protested, hating the almost-whine in her voice. "I don't know what else we could be doing to—"

Dr. Brook held up a hand. "This has absolutely nothing to do with the job you have done as parents. She simply has not had a family for the majority of her life. Even though she calls you Mama and Papa, she doesn't know what it means to have a mother and father—people who care for, nurture, and protect her. In her mind and in her experience, she's alone."

"But we've tried so hard," Julie said, looking at Mark for support. "We adopted her, and we love her—we really do. We . . ." Julie's voice trailed off.

"I know," said Dr. Brook, "and I commend you for what you've done. You are true champions for wanting to give an abandoned child a good family and life, and I deeply admire you for that. You are both extremely well-intentioned, and again, these events have happened through no fault of your own. It is important that you realize we have to try to look at Alina's version of self, others, and the world through *her* eyes—and given what she experienced the first five years of her life, plus all the question marks, it is not reasonable to expect a dramatic turnaround in six months. It's going to take time for her to heal, Mr. and Mrs. Ryan."

Mark and Julie sat in silence, not holding hands, feeling their own pain.

"I'm a dad, Dr. Brook," Mark said finally, stiffly. "Like a lot of dads out there, if I've got a problem, I want to know what it is and how I can fix it. Can you just tell us what all this means? How do I fix my family and take care of my little girl?" Mark's eyes shone with tears. Julie looked away.

"At this point," Dr. Brook said, "after reviewing records, testing, interviews, observation, and completing rating scales and questionnaires, I believe that Alina meets the diagnostic criteria for reactive attachment disorder."

Julie's heart thudded. "What does that mean? Reactive attachment disorder? I've heard of it on some of the international adoption sites, but I don't know much about it."

Dr. Brook passed her a photocopied page. "This is the diagnostic criteria for reactive attachment disorder from the *Diagnostic and Statistical Manual of Mental Disorders – Fourth Edition*," she said. "Reactive attachment disorder—or RAD—is described as a pattern of 'markedly disturbed and developmentally inappropriate social relatedness in most contexts, beginning before five years old.'"

Julie and Mark read the paper they shared between them. The "developmentally inappropriate social relatedness" could be evidenced by a persistent failure to initiate or respond in a developmentally appropriate fashion to most social interactions, as manifested by excessively inhibited, hypervigilant, or highly ambivalent and contradictory responses—such as responding to caregivers with a mixture of approach, avoidance, and resistance to comforting—or may exhibit frozen watchfulness. Or there might be indiscriminate sociability with marked inability to exhibit appropriate selective attachments (evidenced by excessive familiarity with relative strangers, for example, or lack of selectivity in choice of attachment figures).

"Well, Alina definitely seems to meet the criteria for the first part—the one about being inhibited, and a mixture of approach, avoidance, and resistance to comforting." Mark sighed and looked at the floor.

"So all of this," Julie added, "is because she didn't have that initial attachment and bond with a caregiver at the orphanage?"

"Yes," Dr. Brook said. "We don't know what happened at the orphanage. But given her presentation, I would suspect the presence of what is referred to as pathogenic care. That could mean the continued neglect of a child's basic physical needs; disregard for her emotional needs for comfort, stimulation, or affection; and frequent caregiver changes that negatively affected the development of stable attachment patterns."

"So you're saying that Alina was not born this way," Mark said, "but was created this way by the world?"

Dr. Brook gave a regretful nod. "I am, yes. While she was born with her own strengths and challenges—like the rest of us, might I add—her development and brain functioning was directly influenced by her environment, which we know is the case in children who have experienced complex developmental trauma."

"Where does the trauma aspect come in?" Mark asked, bracing himself.

"Well, 'trauma' has been generally viewed as extreme stress—threat to life, bodily integrity, or sanity—that overwhelms a person's ability to cope. If Alina experienced something traumatic—whether that was neglect or physical, emotional, or sexual abuse—her primary emotions were helplessness, vulnerability, and fear. More recently," Dr. Brook continued, "many mental health professionals want to expand the recognition of the impact of interpersonal and attachment trauma that occurs early in life that may not necessarily meet this more standard criteria for trauma."

"What do you mean?" Julie asked. She forced herself to blink past the image of an infant Alina, who was robbed of the experience of feeling safe and loved.

"This literature is informed by the work of Dr. Bessel A. van der Kolk," Dr. Brook said, writing his name down for the Ryans. "He and many others believe that if we look at this through the lens of complex and developmental trauma, multiple exposures to interpersonal trauma—such as abandonment, betrayal, physical or sexual assaults, coercive practices, emotional abuse, or witnessing violence—early in life create intense effects in the child. The child might experience and display a sense of rage, betrayal, fear, resignation, and shame, as well as efforts to ward off the recurrence of these emotions. These kids then often have a pattern of dysregulation in the presence of trauma cues—difficulties may be seen in their affective responses, behavior, thinking, and relational responses. We also often see altered attributions and expectancies such as distrust of caregivers, loss of expectancy of protection by others, and a belief that future victimization is inevitable."

The calm, regular ticking of the wall clock in Dr. Brook's office was the only sound for a few moments as Julie and

Mark let her words sink in. This *lens*, as Dr. Brook called it, cast Alina's behavior in a light that made terrible sense.

"So if I leave her room at night, for example," Julie ventured, "she thinks I'm abandoning her forever. Or if Luke accidentally steps on her toe, she feels she's being physically threatened."

Dr. Brook nodded. "Possibly. Children like Alina may become fearful or enraged in reaction to situations that would have little impact on securely attached children. They may have extreme difficulty returning to a calm state and may develop a world-view that projects their pain and hurt. Often, they expect the trauma to recur, so they act to ward it off, misinterpreting events and experiencing a deep loss of trust in others."

"This is one awful disorder," Mark said, rubbing his temples. He felt a twist of hopelessness in his gut. How were they supposed to counteract the effects of what Alina had been through? How were they supposed to reverse the damage?

"Actually, a knowledgeable colleague of mine believes that the effects of complex trauma are not a 'disorder,'" Dr. Brook said. "More accurately, they represent an 'adaptation.'"

"What do you mean?" Julie asked.

"In overly technical terms, neglect or abuse often results in the over-pruning of the synapses in the right orbitofrontal cortex. In understandable terms, the child's brain changes early in development. In an adaptive and, I want to emphasize, *intelligent way*, her brain reconfigured itself for survival."

"At the expense of relationships with others," Mark said.

Dr. Brook gave a regretful nod. "Survival is primary from an evolutionary perspective, and her brain directed itself toward three useful survival mechanisms: fight, flight, or freeze."

Julie pulled opened to a blank page in her binder and took quick notes as Dr. Brook spoke. As overwhelmed as she felt, there was no way she'd remember everything otherwise.

"Dr. Daniel Siegel does a great job of explaining this phenomena. In flight, the lower brain stem takes over. There's no conscious thought here as we understand it, no logical processing. Reducing threat is the only way to calm," Dr. Brook explained. "Flight can be physical—actually running away—or disassociating in order to feel less helpless. Freezing is exactly what it sounds like: stopping, trying not to exist, ignoring any questions or commands.

"Kids who have experienced complex trauma perceive others and the world as a dangerous place—logically so, because it *has* been truly dangerous, and we are all biologically driven to survive. Essentially, they are constantly in this survival mode. If someone bumps into us at the grocery store, for example, our first response is that it's an accident. But these kids might see it as a threat and go into fight, flight, or freeze."

Julie's hand shook as she wrote. She felt a surge of rage toward whomever had hurt her daughter, whomever had forced her brain to change, forced her to adapt in order to survive as a child. No child deserved this! And what about the others at the orphanage—at all the orphanages across the world? Was this happening there as well? Did those kids turn out like this, too? Was it just Russia, or was it also China or maybe even the United States?

What was happening, and how could people stop it?

"Is there anything we can do?" Mark asked fiercely. "I mean, this can't be permanent, can it?"

Dr. Brook removed her glasses and looked directly at the Ryans. "I think that given Alina's history and the interpersonal trauma she experienced, she will always have some struggles. However, with the right kind of intervention and support, she could make some significant gains. So things *can* get better. For example, I believe it is possible to reduce the intensity and frequency of her meltdowns, improve her social emotional skills, and increase her overall capacities to relate, communicate, and think. We've spoken about this before, but it's important that when Alina starts school, you make a referral for an IEP team evaluation."

"What do we need to do?" asked Julie.

"You should give them a copy of my evaluation, and I can also attend the IEP meeting if you'd like. I also recommend you contact the county's department of human services for additional help."

"We also heard that from Dr. Jenkins," Mark said. "We'll do that."

"Here's the most important thing." Dr. Brook gave Julie and Mark a long, almost stern look. "From this point forward, you are not just Alina's parents. You are her advocates. Her champions. She needs you."

Julie's chest felt tight as a sail stretched by the wind. Dr. Brook's words struck her in a way that ignited her passion: they *were* Alina's advocates. Her champions. They were the only people in the world who would fight for this child, and the overwhelming anxiety they felt couldn't compare to Alina's constant state of vulnerability and fear. Dr. Brook was right: their daughter needed them.

"What should we do first?" Mark asked, as if reading Julie's mind. "I need to do something so I don't feel so helpless."

"Right now, continue with the medication, monitored by a child psychiatrist, and start individual sessions with someone with a background in complex trauma. You need someone who can form a supportive and therapeutic relationship with Alina and who can work with you on behavioral strategies in a trauma-sensitive manner. You are going to make a special education referral, so you should familiarize yourselves with IDEA, or the Individuals with Disabilities Education Act. The law states that *every child* is entitled to a free appropriate education. That means that if Alina qualifies as a student with special education needs, the local school district is legally obligated to provide her with an individualized education plan so she can benefit from her educational program."

"Okay," Mark said, "that's good to know." He looked at Julie, who was scribbling furiously. "Are you getting all this, Jules?"

Julie nodded without looking up. "What is the process for all this?" she asked.

"The school district will have some forms to sign, and then a team of professionals at the school—probably the classroom teacher, school psychologist, school social worker, and maybe a teacher with more specialized training—will evaluate Alina within ninety days from the time of the referral. They will then schedule an IEP meeting, which you—and I, at your request—will attend. If she qualifies for services, then the district, with your input, will develop an individualized educational plan for your daughter that outlines any services, modifications, and accommodations necessary for her to benefit from her educational program. Over the years, I've found that the most important part is making the referral, because once the process starts, it moves along fairly quickly."

"Why is making the referral so hard?" asked Mark.

"The actual referral is easy. But let's just say that I have found some districts somewhat reluctant to initiate one," Dr. Brook said, "especially for a child new to the district."

"Why is that?" asked Mark.

"My own view is that sometimes it comes down to resources—personnel and work responsibilities, state and federal budget cuts, that kind of thing. However, it is important in a case like Alina's that she receive services as soon as possible if she qualifies, so my recommendation to you is to recognize that it is your *right* to make a referral. If you are persistent, assertive, and educated on the law, it will be fine."

Julie and Mark nodded.

After a few more minutes, the meeting ended and the Ryans thanked Dr. Brook. Julie found herself leaning toward Dr. Brook, giving the older woman a brief hug.

The sun was setting, and the silence between Julie and Mark was heavy and oppressive as they drove home. Julie thought with bittersweet longing of the first time they'd seen Alina's photo. Would they have gone forward with the adoption if they'd known how their life would change? If they had known the level of constant worry and anxiety? She wanted to think they would have done it all over again, but doubt pulled at her. And now she felt soaked through with grief. She mourned the past, the life

Alina could be living if her basic needs had been met as a baby; she was mourning the present, the family life that felt more extreme every day; and she was mourning the future, which seemed so threatened with struggle and hardship. *Stop it, Julie!* she told herself. *It doesn't have to be this way. Nothing is set; nothing is totally unchangeable. There is always hope.* She let herself feel comforted for a moment.

Mark glanced occasionally at Julie. She was gazing out the window, and a slant of sunlight brightened her hair. He wanted to say something, but he was sifting through numbers in his mind. Though Dr. Brook hadn't mentioned the financial effects of Alina's care, he sensed the sacrifices they would need to make as a family. Alina would need specialized care for a long time, and insurance would only cover a portion, he was sure. And what if she couldn't handle school and had to stay home? What if one of them were forced to leave their job to take care of her? What would happen to their savings? Luke's college fund? Would *Alina* ever go to college or have job? What kind of future would she have as an adult? What would happen to her after Mark and Julie became old or passed away?

Lost in anxious and troubling thoughts, neither of them spoke a word until Mark pulled up the driveway. Then he said, "Let's go for a walk."

Julie was surprised. "But—" She reflexively prepared to argue with her husband.

"Your mother can watch her for a few more minutes. It'll be fine, Julie."

She bit her lip but nodded. Without speaking, they walked away from their house, and Julie kept time to

Mark's steps until she realized where they were heading: a little park a few blocks away, tucked into the trees and empty most of the time. When Julie was pregnant with Luke, they used to take dinner there and sit beside each other on the children's swings that made them feel like giants. Their toes had scuffed the gravel as they pushed themselves gently, talking about what life might be like once the baby came. Then when Luke was born, Julie had taken him there during the day, when she needed to get out of the house but was exhausted by the thought of navigating car seats and strollers. And as he grew, he went there with his neighborhood friends. It had been years since Julie and Mark had been at the park together.

They settled into their familiar swings, chains squeaking, and Julie closed her eyes as the early fall breeze lifted the hair off her neck.

"We need a plan," Mark said. "It seems like we've been either isolating ourselves or attacking each other ever since we brought Alina home, and it has to stop. We'll go crazy otherwise."

"Speak for yourself," Julie said, eyes still closed. "I'm already there."

Mark gave a half-hearted laugh before a feeling of heaviness overtook him. "It sounds like the first thing we have to do, while we get a referral underway, is call the county and see about those services Dr. Jenkins and Dr. Brook mentioned. God knows, anything would help us right now."

"Mark," Julie said.

"Yeah?"

"It's so hard for me to love her." Julie's voice broke with the shame of her admission. She hardly dared look at her husband, who sighed beside her. "I want to—I want to so badly, and I *do*, but sometimes . . . I swear, Mark, sometimes I wish she were somebody else's child."

"I know," he said. "I know. But we are all she has."

"I know." Julie pushed herself higher on the swing, exhaling every time the swing arced downward. She'd never before felt this true *burden* of parenthood—the burden that no matter what she felt in her heart, she would sacrifice everything for her child. "We'll just have to work harder. We'll get through this."

"We have to," Mark said. "There's no other option."

CHAPTER 13
A CHANCE FOR SOME RESPITE?

Early the next morning, Julie researched online for the county department of human services. She called and was eventually connected to a "child services care coordinator," a social worker who agreed to meet with them the following week to discuss Alina's case. Julie and Mark spent the week wondering how to prepare for the visit. They felt it was a critical point but didn't know what to do to ready themselves.

The care coordinator's name was Carol, and they spoke several times on the phone before she visited the Ryans' house. Carol was around Julie's age with long straight hair and a mildly lined face bare of any makeup. Julie felt flustered and awkward, dropping Carol's jacket on the way to the living room and chattering too quickly for it to sound natural. Mark gave her one of his patented "you're talking too much" glances, but Julie was all nerves and couldn't change her desperate desire to make a good impression. *Though what would making a good impression do?* she thought. *We're calling the county because we need help, not to prove we're fine.*

"Can I get you anything to drink?" she asked. "Water,

lemonade, juice? I'd offer you a soda, but we're trying to stay away from all the sugar, but oh! We do have coffee or tea if you'd prefer?"

Carol smiled. "A glass of water would be great. Thank you."

Mark excused himself to get the water, and Julie and Carol settled onto two chairs in the living room.

"You can't tell," Julie said, gesturing to the beige slip-covers on which they sat, "but these chairs are actually antiques. They were my grandmother's. But you know, with Alina, we have to be careful . . ."

Carol looked around the living room, and Julie saw it through her eyes: the coffee table and side tables bare of books, picture frames, or knickknacks; the bookshelves with all the bottom shelves empty; dents in the wall where items had flown; a large, watery-looking crack on the corner of the flatscreen TV.

Carol smiled sympathetically. "It seems like your hands are pretty full, Julie."

The brief, genuine moment of understanding was all Julie needed. In seconds, she was telling Carol about Alina's rages and diagnoses of a mood disorder, oppositional defiant disorder, and now reactive attachment disorder; the psychiatric hospitalization and medication; and the developmental delays.

"The psychologist, Dr. Brook, said you might be able to provide some help—she called it *respite*," Julie said. "Is there anything you can do to help us? Our marriage is solid, but we are struggling."

"You and I have talked quite a bit over the past week, I've asked a lot of questions, and I've also managed to read all the records you sent me. From what I'm hearing,"

Carol said, "Alina meets the criteria for Wraparound Milwaukee's REACH program. REACH is a family-centered, team approach that pairs a care coordinator—in your case, me—with a family. We help connect parents with additional resources and provide individualized care to youth who have been diagnosed with a serious mental disturbance, are in two or more service systems, and demonstrate behavior that is compromising safety at home and at school. As an organization, our goal is to eventually get you to a place where you don't need us anymore." She smiled.

Mark, who had handed Carol a glass of water, sat down next to Julie and nodded. "That's what we want. We need all this help—but I don't *want* all this help, if that makes sense," he said. "We just want some normalcy. Our son, Luke—as much as we're suffering, he's the one I feel for the most. Luke didn't choose any of this, and as unfair as it was for Alina to have experienced whatever she did, it's unfair for Luke to be going through this as well. It's hard for me to not feel like we've completely screwed up our parenting duties for our son."

Julie cringed, but Carol nodded. "You're not the only parents to tell me that. Your family is in a tough spot, Mark. You have a child who has experienced complex trauma, which is awful to think about in individual cases and even worse to consider as a worldwide phenomenon. While Alina is from Russia, complex trauma is not limited to that country or anywhere else. We see it all over, unfortunately, and all we can do is try to lessen its effects."

"Why does this happen, though?" asked Julie. "How could someone have a baby and . . . ?"

"I've been doing this job for ten years, and I don't know," Carol answered. "That's a question probably best left for philosophers, sociologists, and religion to answer—how and why this happens to some children and not others. What I do know is that we have a little girl to help—so let's talk more about Alina, okay?"

After another half hour, Carol left them with some forms to sign and a parent handbook for the program. She told them they would need to set up their next meeting within the following thirty days to put together a plan that would involve services the REACH program could "buy" from an integrated provider network, as well as free or funded outside resources. Changes to the plan, Carol explained, would be made at least once every three months.

"We'll review everything tonight and get back to you with any questions by tomorrow," Julie said.

"Take your time," Carol said at the door. "Make sure you understand everything."

Julie and Mark exchanged glances. What they understood was that there was no time to waste. They sent the paperwork in the following day, and a meeting was scheduled for two weeks later.

Over the next six months, Carol came to the house once a month to support the family and visit with Alina. Mark and Julie used that time to take Luke out, if he accepted the invitation, or go to the movies on their own. Once, they rented a hotel room, peeled back the comforter on a king-sized bed, and just slept. There was some improvement in Alina's language and communication skills, but even with the help of the REACH program, her behavior continued to be consistently challenging, marked by frequent and intense times of high agitation. Julie and Mark often walked around dazed, wondering where they were going, and bit by bit continued to box and hide anything Alina might throw or destroy. Their house had assumed the barren look of one in the early stages of moving, all personal touches gone, an air of loss. Luke hated being home and spent as much time as he could with relatives or friends. Julie would never say it out loud, but she was glad Luke was out of the house more often. She saw the look in his eyes when Alina raged—a mixture of powerlessness, fear, and anger—and with him out of the house, she had one less child to worry about. She knew her entire family would feel the consequences later. Without a doubt, Luke felt as cast away as he'd feared he would be when he was seven years old and first saw Alina's picture. Even with the additional support, Julie felt that her family's situation was desperate.

At six and a half years old, Alina should have been in first grade, but Julie and Mark were all too aware of how far behind she was. Plus, they were fearful about how school would proceed for Alina and the challenges that would entail. When early August came, they enrolled her in first grade and, armed with recommendations from both Dr. Jenkins and Dr. Brook, requested an IEP team evaluation for special education.

"How long has Alina been in the States?" asked Mrs. Adams, the school principal. She was in her fifties, with gray-threaded hair pulled back into a low chignon. She sat across her desk from them in an office that smelled of books, coffee, and the sharp hint of permanent marker.

Julie looked at Mark. "Let's see—about a year and a half now?"

Mark exhaled and shook his head. "If you'd asked me, I would have said five years."

Mrs. Adams looked between them, and Julie forced a smile. "We've had a bit of a difficult time adjusting to having Alina in our home," she explained. She wasn't sure why she made such a drastic understatement.

"You have to understand," Mrs. Adams said, "I hear what you're telling me about the doctors' diagnoses and recommendations, but your daughter hasn't even been in school yet. Identifying a student to have a special education disability is quite significant, and we'd like to have a period of time to see how she adjusts to the school setting and interventions in regular education. Why don't you give me all of her records and I'll stay in close touch with her teacher about her behavior. We'll just take things step by step." Mrs. Adams smiled and rose from her seat. "We're looking forward to seeing Alina when the school year starts."

"Wait," Mark said. "That's it? You're saying no to evaluating her?"

"Not at all," Mrs. Adams said. "I'm just asking for patience on your part as we observe how she does here on her own. In the meantime, if you're willing, I'm planning on asking our school psychologist to meet with you for some non-special education assessment so we can complete some behavior rating scales on Alina. This will give us some good information on strengths and weaknesses for intervention planning if that becomes necessary."

Julie looked at Mark, then back at Mrs. Adams. "Mrs. Adams, there's no way Alina can be in a regular education classroom right now. Trust us. I wish she could, but she's been through so much, and her behavior is—"

"I understand all that, ma'am," Mrs. Adams said. "And believe me, we'll take everything into consideration. We take our obligations to students with potential special education needs seriously. We just need some time to see how Alina adjusts and to gauge her progress."

She handed Julie and Mark some forms to sign for Alina's enrollment, as well as an agreement to complete the behavior rating scales for the school psychologist. *Paperwork, that's all we get*, thought Julie, *and promises of help, but no real help right now.* Julie took the forms and slipped them into her "Alina binder."

Mrs. Adams touched Julie's shoulder as she walked them to the door and offered a gentle smile. "I want you to know we're on your side."

"Of course you are," said Julie, struggling to keep the bitterness from her voice.

CHAPTER 14
SCHOOL

Months passed quickly—more quickly than Julie had anticipated—and soon Alina's first term in first grade raced to a close. There had been one "Collaborative Support Team" meeting after another, in which Mark and Julie met with Mrs. Adams, Alina's teacher—whom Alina called "Ms. Natalie"—and the school psychologist—to discuss Alina's behavior. The meetings were difficult to schedule, however, because the school psychologist, Mr. House, worked at three different schools in the district. In the plan that the team developed, Julie and Mark received a daily report from Ms. Natalie with Alina's behavior represented in stickers: super smiley face, smiley face, neutral face, and sad face. The school talked about things like "replacement behaviors" and ignoring Alina when she threw tantrums instead of giving her attention during those times. They reinforced good behavior with stickers and small pieces of candy. Alina seemed to like some of the stickers and, of course, the candy, but Julie wasn't convinced she was learning how to handle frustration or deal with transitions better by earning stickers and candy.

The best part about school was that Alina seemed to like Ms. Natalie. Alina hovered close by her in the classroom, nodding or shaking her head to simple questions. Ms. Natalie was a compassionate mother of two in her mid-thirties who had taken a special interest in Alina. She offered as much one-on-one instruction and attention as she could with a classroom of twenty-five children, often reading from small books with one or two words per page and encouraging Alina to repeat them. This support complemented the assistance Alina was receiving through a county behavior therapist who came to the house once per week. Julie swelled with pride when Alina opened one of her small books, pointed to a picture of a cow, and said, "Cow."

Problems in the classroom arose when Ms. Natalie shifted her attention from Alina to another student, or when one of the other kids did something Alina interpreted as aggressive or hostile, such as taking one of her toys or accidentally bumping into her. Though she rarely raged in school, she did lapse into the "frozen" component of the fight, flight, or freeze response that Dr. Brook had mentioned. Ms. Natalie called these times "passive noncompliance," wherein Alina would shut down and not respond to adult requests for an extended period of time. It was as though she entirely folded in on herself, trying to become invisible and unreachable—to disappear. Julie could tell when this happened by Alina's presence after school; there were days when she seemed, in a very real sense, *absent* when she followed Julie into the car.

At home, some days were better than others. The start of the day often indicated how it would finish, while the finish of one day hinted at the start of the next morning.

If Alina met Julie's eyes in the morning with that heart-breakingly sweet smile, then she would follow Julie's urging to get out of bed. And if she rose from bed and walked with Julie into the bathroom, she would listen to Julie's patient instructions to "peepee in the potty," lowering her pull-ups and sitting on the potty-training toilet they had placed next to the regular one. And if she did *that*, she would sit for breakfast, let Julie place her pill under her tongue, drink some water to wash the medication down, and eventually be ready for school.

If school went badly, Alina's sense of absence afterward might shift into rage and fury at the slightest provocation at home: a dinner plate removed before she was ready, even if she weren't eating; Luke refusing to relinquish the TV remote; or Julie telling her it was time for a bath. The rages could last into the night hours, when Julie tearfully told Mark to just go to bed because she'd be sleeping in Alina's room. Then, the next morning, if Alina refused to make eye contact with Julie when she went to wake her for school, it was a pretty certain sign that the day was lost already to Alina's unassailable anger. On those days, Julie called the school and, feeling deeply and utterly like a failure, said that Alina was not feeling well and would be back at school the next day. Then she called work and let them know she would need to take another personal day. The sympathetic understanding in her supervisor's voice had changed to neutrality, and Julie was sure that would soon change to tension, and then finally, to anger. He had a company to run, after all, and employees always calling in for personal days was not good. All in all, the situation was untenable. Alina was just getting by in school, the family was just getting by at home, and

Julie and Mark were just getting by at work. Julie was also thinking that she and Mark were just getting by in their marriage. Something needed to change. Soon.

They called Carol, the county social worker, toward the end of one of Alina's meltdowns. It had been six hours, and Julie was exhausted from begging, cajoling, threatening, and crying. Mark had long since taken Luke to a friend's house, and when he returned, eyes red-rimmed and face blotchy with stress, Alina was finally calm—sitting, arms crossed, glaring at the television.

Carol arrived the next morning and met with the Ryans. She was irritated, but not entirely surprised, when told that Alina had not yet been formally evaluated for special education. She immediately put them in touch with Mr. Marshall, a special education advocate through REACH with twenty years of experience. He would work on behalf of Alina and her parents in their interaction with the school district.

In March, two years since bringing Alina home, the Ryans—with Mr. Marshall's assistance—again requested a special education evaluation for Alina at a Collaborative Support Team meeting. The team—including the Ryans, Mr. Marshall, Mrs. Adams, Mr. House, and Ms. Natalie— met to discuss Alina's progress in the classroom. They sat in a small conference room off the main office, with students glancing curiously through the window as they scurried with bright backpacks to class.

This time, Ms. Natalie was a vocal part of the conversation, stating that Alina demonstrated significant emotional and behavioral concerns in the classroom that required additional services and supports beyond those found in regular education.

"It's clear to me that Alina performs best when she receives more focused adult interaction and attention," Ms. Natalie said. She pushed her curly brown hair behind her ears when she spoke, delivering her input with confidence. "When she's having a bad day in school, much like the Ryans have said, she shuts down, becomes irritable, and can be explosive. There is little my aide and I can do to support her when I have twenty-five other students who need my attention. She's made some slight behavioral gains with our behavioral plans and sticker charts, but she seems to have learning problems and special education needs that should be evaluated by the school district. This could be even more important next year when, if what the papers say is true, there will be budget cuts and *thirty* kids to a class with no aide. I absolutely think we should make a referral for an IEP team evaluation."

Mr. Marshall, the special education advocate, who had been sitting quietly through the discussion, smiled at Ms. Natalie. "I agree," he said simply.

Julie almost crumpled with gratitude. Though Mrs. Adams had been polite and always willing to talk, hearing Ms. Natalie's perspective was the first time she felt they had a true advocate for Alina in the school system.

After more discussion, Ms. Adams agreed that while some minor gains had been made with the regular education school-based approaches, it was time for an IEP team evaluation due to a suspected special education need in the area of emotional behavioral disability. The Ryans signed paperwork and consent forms for testing by the IEP team, which initiated the ninety-day timeline Dr. Brook had referenced.

Over the next two months, the school psychologist completed a series of observations, parent and teacher interviews, classroom observations, parent and teacher behavior rating scales, and individual testing with Alina. Meanwhile, the school social worker, Ms. English, visited the Ryans' home and obtained home, community, and developmental information. Finally, the team evaluation was scheduled for a Tuesday in early April.

The IEP team was comprised of Julie and Mark, Mrs. Adams, Mr. House, Ms. English, Mr. Marshall, and—at the Ryans' request—Dr. Brook. The team reviewed all the findings, including history, psychological and hospital reports, interviews, observations, and current testing results. Unequivocally, they found that Alina was exhibiting significant social, emotional, and behavioral difficulties that departed from generally accepted norms and adversely affected her academic progress, social relationships, personal adjustment, and classroom adjustment. The team also determined that Alina was demonstrating severe, chronic, and frequent behavioral problems in the school and home setting. She was also showing an inability to develop satisfactory interpersonal relationships and demonstrating inappropriate affective or behavioral responses to normal situations. After some discussion, the IEP members were in agreement that Alina met the criteria for emotional behavior disability and required participation in special education in order to benefit from her education.

Julie and Mark exchanged a glance loaded with triumph and relief. This felt like a first battle won.

After determining that Alina met the criteria for emotional behavior disability, the team members talked more about Alina, her behavior, and how they might be able to help through the IEP. Dr. Brook said, "When we think of behavior, it's important to consider what skills are lacking or getting in the way of more socially adaptive behavior. In Alina's case, I think we need to remember that she struggles with understanding, expressing, and modulating her emotions. She doesn't yet have the language to express her thoughts and emotions adequately in words, which can be frustrating. When we factor in her low frustration threshold and difficulty regulating emotions, we have a perfect storm for classroom disruption and poor learning. She also has some social skill deficits, such as difficulty reading social cues and not understanding how to connect with others.

"One of the biggest difficulties I see, though," Dr. Brook continued, looking around the room, "is Alina's difficulties with cognitive inflexibility—she is a quite literal, black and white thinker. She struggles to shift mindset and adapt to changes in the environment. This may mean something as simple as a change in school activity or class, or a change in the people around her—in this case, going from Ms. Natalie, whom she knows, to a new teacher, who will be unfamiliar. These changes require adjustment and also trust—something challenging for her. We have to remember that the effects of early interpersonal and complex trauma are deep. For Alina, every transition reenacts the original loss."

Dr. Brook's words weighed heavily on the room. Everyone was silent around the conference table. They considered how unfair the world had been to Alina and how much she had lost so early in her life. The original loss— the loss of her mother, the loss of her basic needs being met, the loss of early parent attachment and bonding, the loss of a real childhood based upon trusting other people. Julie's heart hurt. Again, she felt the injustice of Alina's situation. This was not a life path that Alina chose; these were not thoughts, emotions, or reactions that she decided to possess. Julie understood this now, and she vowed to remind herself of that in the times of anger toward Alina—even the times she felt Alina was being manipulative and controlling.

With Dr. Brook's guidance, the IEP team discussed the framework of the program and then scheduled a follow-up meeting a week later to develop the final IEP. Prior to the meeting, Julie spent her lunch breaks and evenings poring over the State Board of Education and Department of Public Instruction websites to learn more about special education and the development of an IEP. There was an overwhelming amount of information online, but the key to success as Julie understood it was to assemble a strong team—a group of people that Julie believed were committed to helping Alina succeed in school. In Alina's case, this would include the people at the table for the team evaluation meeting, as well as the new special education teacher. Together, the group would design Alina's special education plan, including academic and behavioral goals and objectives.

The IEP team met exactly a week after the evaluation meeting to discuss, develop, and finalize the annual education program for Alina. Julie and Mark found the meeting to be long—over two hours—and fairly difficult to follow with all the forms and language but were overall pleased with the way the school appreciated their input and perspective. Of course, Julie was also frustrated that it had taken so long for Alina to qualify for services when her daughter's needs seemed so obvious. However, she chose to be grateful and hopeful rather than focus on the negative.

"If we could dream for her," Julie said softly in bed that night, "if we could reach inside her and just . . . change or rearrange things, what would we do? What do we want for her?"

Mark sighed and shifted beneath the blankets, pulling Julie close and resting his chin on the top of her head. Julie smiled in the darkness. This was how they'd always slept in college, until Mark's arm inevitably fell asleep and he rolled away. These days, they were so exhausted that if they slept in the same bed, at the same time, they fell into deep solitary sleeps with a yawning gap between them.

"I want her to learn to trust people," Mark said. "Not everyone is worthy of trust, I know, but let's start with us. I think if she can learn to trust us, a lot of other things will fall into place. Maybe she wouldn't melt down at any change—or not as bad, if she trusted or believed that not every change necessarily means some kind of loss."

Julie was surprised at the passion in Mark's voice, the depth of his emotion. She knew he loved Alina, of course, but Mark—like most men—was a man who wanted to take action. When confronted with a problem, he wanted to know how to fix it. He was a solutions-oriented man who had less interest in overly analyzing a problem than he did in devising a way to change it. In these moments, Julie felt closer to her husband than she had in months.

"So we want to improve her ability to trust others," Julie said. "And when I think about her future, I also think about her basic life skills. I want her to be as independent as she possibly can be one day. I don't know if that'll happen the same way it will for Luke, but for now, I want her to not be so dependent on us."

"The diapers," Mark said.

"The diapers," Julie repeated, cringing. "Although, to be fair, she is using pull-ups and pottying half the time."

"Half the time?" Mark asked. "That's great. Nice going, Jules."

Julie smiled, pleased at Mark's recognition of her efforts. "Setting an alarm, getting out of bed," she continued, "getting dressed, keeping a personal self-care routine, having good nutrition, being safe. God, Mark—she's such a paradox. As guarded and wary as she always is, she is also often entirely unaware of real life dangers. She doesn't seem to realize she could die if she throws a car door open when we're driving, and I can see her easily wandering off one day in search of bugs, and then what?"

Mark wrapped a hand around the back of Julie's neck, extending his fingers into her hair and rubbing her scalp. After a long, contemplative pause, in which everything unsaid did not go unfelt, he said, "We need to remember what we heard from Dr. Brook. We are her advocates now." Julie nodded. The darkness, Mark's fingers gently kneading her scalp, the quiet rise and fall of their voices—just a little, just for a moment, while the world was quiet and Alina wasn't screaming "Mama!" . . . she let herself feel hope.

CHAPTER 15
SPECIAL CLASS

Alina remembered Ms. Natalie. Ms. Natalie in front of the classroom, hair curly and brown like tree bark. Ms. Natalie smiling down, saying, "Alina, why don't we read a little?" Sitting in the corner, leaning on a shiny yellow beanbag chair, looking at a picture book. Ms. Natalie's hands with the yellow ring and pink nails, pointing, saying words. "Dog. Cat. Duck. Cow." Pointing at symbols, lines, some straight and some squiggly. "This is the alphabet. This is the letter A . . ."

Some words, some English, Alina was starting to understand. Not just sounds, noise, anymore. Mama, in the morning, showing Alina pictures.

"See this? This is Alina getting out of bed. See the smile? Alina is happy to get out of bed. That's what we're about to do."

Following Mama to bathroom.

"See this one? This is Alina going to the potty like a big girl."

Alina getting ready for a shower; Alina putting her arms in a sweater; Alina at the breakfast table; Alina in the car. All the way to school, pictures. Matching words:

bed, smile, potty, shower, breakfast, school.

But now school was different. Alina was in different classroom. No more Ms. Natalie. One day, everything changed. Small class and three other kids.

"One . . . two . . . three," said Alina's new teacher. Mama said this was Alina's "special class." *Special.* Just a sound, still. Alina missed Ms. Natalie. Didn't understand where she went. Felt . . . hot, scared, confused thinking of her gone.

"We can go back and visit Ms. Natalie," Mama said. "You're just moving a little down the hallway. See?"

Ms. Natalie kneeling, looking into Alina's eyes. Alina was mad. Turned her head away, arms crossed. Didn't want to be here.

"Alina?" Ms. Natalie. "I'm close by if you need anything. I'll come check on you, okay?"

Alina silent. Heart pounding. She knew; she always knew. No one stayed.

CHAPTER 16
PLODDING FORWARD

Alina's IEP specified that she would work in a special-ized classroom, almost at a one-to-one adult to student ratio, to build specific academic and behavioral skills. It was heartbreaking to take her out of Ms. Natalie's class; Alina sometimes still randomly asked, "Ms. Natalie?" and looked at Julie with such bafflement and hurt that it made Julie want to weep.

"You're going to have some new teachers, honey," Julie told Alina. Alina stared back, the hurt in her eyes eventu-ally giving way to emptiness.

Julie understood what the change in teachers meant for Alina. Her daughter had developed trust and be-come attached to Ms. Natalie. Securely attached kids could more easily develop trusting relationships; while people-changes were sometimes difficult for them, too, they were more resilient and equipped to adapt to those changes than children with attachment difficulties. "Moving on" looked different from the eyes of a child with attachment issues. In Alina's mind, Ms. Natalie was able to read her cues. She was supportive, nurturant, and developmentally appropriate; she provided certainty, consistency, and stability; most importantly, she believed that Alina wanted to do well, despite the challenging behavior she often displayed. While Ms. Natalie was Alina's teacher, she had also become something much more: a responsive, supportive, trustworthy, and compassionate adult in her life. And now Julie and Mark were forcing her to walk away. Julie couldn't help worrying that Alina would later blame them, and she lost sleep imagining the ways in which her daughter might express that anger.

Still, whatever suffering there might be in the short term, Julie and Mark were certain that the smaller class size and the increased attention and instruction from a special education teacher with a background in emotional and behavioral disabilities was what Alina needed. She had also been receiving English as a Second Language services and meeting with the school psychologist twice a week for social skills and to learn how to better understand and express emotions. While her English comprehension and minimal reading skills were improving, the school counseling sessions didn't seem to be helping much. Alina rarely openly raged at school, but if her mood darkened, she continued to defy her teachers with silence and stillness.

"We've been trying to engage Alina in schoolwork by using hands-on learning activities, which she seems to enjoy," said her new teacher, "but it hasn't worked well. She's not being disruptive, but she refuses to work. We've also been trying to get her out to the playground more during recess, but we're not pushing it."

Julie sighed. Anytime the phone rang during the day, she cringed. The "bad day" phone calls were fairly regular, and she knew they would often lead to worse nights.

All she could do was maximize the time she had at work and with Luke. "Well, she can sit there and pout all day if she likes," Julie said, keeping her voice low at her desk, trying not to draw attention to herself. "If she acts up, call me. Otherwise, I'll be there for her at two-thirty."

At home, Alina's behavior was unpredictable. Luke hated being there, and Julie couldn't blame him; home was the kingdom where Alina's moods reigned, putting the rest of them at the mercy of a tiny seven-year-old girl. Julie felt they were all wires with the plastic coating frayed off, metal that sparked at the lightest touch. Then one day the wires exploded: Julie found out she was pregnant.

CHAPTER 17
BABY

Mama getting bigger. Stomach tight and round under flowered dresses. Mama walking funny, with shorter steps, and groaning when she stood up from the couch. Mama said new baby on the way.

"You're going to be a big sister soon," Mama told Alina. On Alina's bed, Mama opened a book. "There's going to be a baby," she read. "When it's ready, in the fall, when the leaves are turning brown and falling . . ." Mama flipped pages. Put Alina's hand on her belly.

"No." Alina drew her hand back. Alina didn't want new baby. Why did Mama and Papa want new baby? Wasn't Alina good enough?

Mama kept growing, but Alina didn't talk about new baby. New baby wasn't coming, couldn't come, if Alina kept saying no. Or if Alina tried to be good. She tried. But sometimes—things she hated. Bells ringing and "Recess is over" and "Oh, Alina, your pockets are filled with dirt" and "It's time for counseling" and "Take your pill" and "Come inside now" and "Alina, give me the remote" and "God, why are you such a freak" and "Alina, it's time to wake up." So many things, and then Alina would be bad.

Times Alina was bad, Mama picked up phone.

"Carol, I'm sorry. Can you come over today and help with Alina? She's raging again, and I can't—okay. An hour? Okay, I'll try."

Then Carol came to the house. Carol. Sometimes they sat together, drew pictures. Alina liked drawing. But sometimes Alina only wanted Mama, not Carol. Why was *Carol* there?

"Mama!" Alina shrieked. Hit Mama's stomach. Mama gasped.

Carol's hands, holding Alina. "Alina, you have to calm down. You can't hit your mom like that; the baby could be hurt. Do you understand? You wouldn't want to hurt your new baby brother or sister, would you?"

"Yes!" Alina yelled. "Hurt baby! Hurt baby!"

CHAPTER 18
911

Margaret was born just after Alina turned eight. Luke was twelve and just as wary of the new addition as Alina. His eyes, once so bright and mischievous, were hooded and dark. He didn't want to hold Margaret; in fact, he hardly looked at her, and he shoved his white iPod earbuds in his ears when she started to cry. Mark was working twelve- to fourteen-hour days, gunning for a promotion that might help augment some of the income they'd lost when Julie resigned from her job. She was only circumventing the inevitable. Her supervisor barely spoke to her, and there was no way she could return to work after a brief maternity leave. Between a crying infant, a sullen preteen, and a demanding Alina, Julie was barely holding on. There were times, when Alina was raging and Margaret was shrieking, that Julie just leaned against the bedroom door and let herself cry as loudly as her daughters were screaming. Their voices mingled together in a chorus of deep unhappiness, and Julie prayed, "Please, please give me strength."

The saving grace was the time Alina spent in school. She had continued to make progress through the supports outlined in the IEP. Though she rarely initiated conversations with adults or peers in school and continued with her passive noncompliance, especially during transitions, she liked her teacher and often spoke in short sentences. During the times she was calm and serene at home, she sat close to Julie on the couch with her head on her shoulder. Sometimes she said softly, "I love you, Mama." Julie's heart felt raw and inflamed during those times, on fire with a mixture of gratitude, love, weariness, and suspicion; did Alina mean what she said? Did she even understand what love meant? Could she feel love? Or was she trying to manipulate Julie somehow?

Carol was another godsend. Though Alina refused to go anywhere with her, she sat and drew and watched TV with Carol during the times she came over. Those brief moments of respite saved Julie's sanity.

"How can you do it?" friends and family asked. The ones who had witnessed Alina's rages were especially disbelieving. "I hate to say it, Jules, but she's not *really* your daughter. You have Luke and now Margaret to think of. Have you ever thought of . . . you know, sending her somewhere? Sending her back?"

"Sending her back?" Julie snapped. "You mean returning her like a television that's not working right? No, I haven't thought of sending her back." *Liar*, hissed a voice deep in her mind. "And Alina is my daughter," Julie added forcefully. How could the people in her life not understand her battle-worn love for this child? How could they not understand that loving Alina was a thing Julie chose to do every day, willingly, the same way she chose to get out of bed when she just wanted to hide beneath the blankets? How could they stand so far away and criticize instead of joining the fray and helping? No one—not a single *one* of Julie's friends—ever offered to watch Alina, giving Julie a moment to remember herself. By the time Margaret was one year old, most of Julie's old friendships were bittersweet memories.

Then, when Alina was ten years old, she hit another wall. She had definitive likes and dislikes in school, gravitating toward activities where she could use her hands and focus intensely on the activity—she liked "science" projects, mostly those involving growing small plants from seeds, and hated reading and other more abstract subjects. She still had little patience for following adult directions, including needing to wait, and her temper had not shown much improvement when she was required to transition between activities. To improve her language and reading skills, her teachers used word games and computer aided instruction. For classroom behavior, Alina had a sticker chart and was given stickers as rewards—shiny gold stars for "Super Duper Effort!" and smiling suns for "Good Work!" Alina loved getting gold stars and said they were "pretty." She lined them up on a laminated chart and often pulled Julie by the hand to see her chart after school. However, on days she misbehaved and was given "Good Work!" or no sticker at all, she raged as if her heart had been freshly broken.

Julie had read all about positive and negative reinforcement on the Internet and learned that kids with attachment issues reacted well to positive reinforcement. More recently, though, it seemed as if positive reinforcement or any positive adult attention made her more upset instead of happier. Plus, Alina had picked up a new habit of wandering off whenever she wanted and to wherever her focus was pulled: a butterfly flitting from bud to bud, a neighbor riding a bike around the corner. Alina had a real and terrifying lack of safety awareness and of the world around her.

Meanwhile, Luke was fourteen and begging Julie and Mark to allow him to get his hardship license. They would have to submit an application, and then—after taking lessons—Luke would be able to drive a car on his own. "You guys are so busy with Alina and Margaret all the time," he argued. "Tell me it wouldn't make life a lot easier for you if you didn't have to be chauffeuring me everywhere?"

He had a point, but Julie refused to admit it. Hardship license? How had that become a valid possibility for their family? She remembered a girl she went to high school with who had her hardship license. The other students looked at her with a mixture of awe and pity as she drove herself to school in an old Chevy Nova, always reeking of cigarette smoke. No one knew what her home life was like, but there was speculation of illness, neglect, and maybe abuse. Now Julie thought, *Perhaps they had a child like Alina.* The problem was that Luke was already not following the weak curfew and rules they set for him. God knew what he would do if he had the freedom of driving a car to suit his moods. "You'll be fifteen in a year," Julie told him, "and then you can take driver's ed with the rest of your friends."

And then there was Margaret. Two years old now, with strawberry blond hair in a shade uncannily similar to Alina's and almond-shaped brown eyes that almost closed when she smiled or laughed. Margaret was a sweet, shy child who hovered close by Julie and Mark and was undeniably and obviously terrified of Alina. Once, Alina had pushed her sister hard into a wall during a rage, and the look of startled hurt in Margaret's eyes was almost worse than the wails when she registered pain. At times of acute paranoia, Julie wondered if they were meeting all of Margaret's basic needs. Was *she* being neglected, in a way? Were they doing their job as parents, or were they so preoccupied with their other daughter that they were unintentionally recreating a similar injustice for Margaret? Thoughts like this paralyzed Julie with worry, hurtling her into a grim vision of the future from which it took focused effort to disengage.

They were caught in a perilous status quo when Alina flew into her worst rage yet—the one with the knife. Alina was no sadist—no "budding psychopath," as Julie had overheard one of the neighbors comment. She didn't enjoy hurting people, and she was sad and seemed to feel remorse afterwards. But when she was trapped in the fury of her rage, she was opportunistic, explosive, and destructive. She seemed to have an intention to hurt. She destroyed property in the home, throwing books at the wall and windows, breaking plates on the wall and floors, and slamming doors over and over. She attacked those close by—so, usually Julie and Mark—by hitting, kicking, and scratching. She screamed and cried, still without tears, hard enough to make her eventually gasp from breathlessness, bringing blood to her nose. Anything to exorcise the enormous depth of feeling in her tiny body, the feeling she still had so little ability to express to the world. And how would they help her find this ability—to tell the world of her pain in a way that didn't bring pain to others?

Julie gasped as Alina headbutted her, catching her cheekbone.

"Mommy?" Margaret called from the base of the stairs. She clutched the telephone in one hand and blanket in another. "Call 9-1-1?"

The darkness in Julie's vision swelled. "Honey, it's okay. Go to your room."

Over Alina's thrashing body, which Julie and Mark could hardly contain, their eyes met again. Blood pooled on his upper lip while sweat made him blink hard. The same desperate question Julie had was reflected in his gaze.

What now?

"I can hold her for a little while," Mark said. "Call MUTT!"

"Are you sure?" Julie managed as Alina threw a vicious kick into Julie's shin.

"Yes! Go! Now!"

Julie let go of Alina's arms and raced to the refrigerator, where the Mobile Urgent Treatment Team number—given to them by Carol as part of the REACH program—was held with a magnet. Julie fumbled the number on her cell phone twice before finally getting it right, and she spewed out such a litany of information and desperation that, after she hung up, she did not remember a word she had said. When the team arrived, she wept in relief that she had given the right address after all.

The rest of the night was a blur. The MUTT personnel transported Alina to the county short-term psychiatric hospital for children, while Mark followed behind and Julie stayed home with Luke and Margaret. Luke's door never even opened, and Julie couldn't be sure he'd heard any of the commotion; it was likely that his headphones were blaring, as they always were these days. Instead, Julie slipped into Margaret's small bed, pressing her face against Margaret's soft hair to keep from screaming. But no matter how hard she tried, Julie could not stop the tears from falling, dampening Margaret's fine-spun curls.

The next day, while Alina was at the hospital, Carol stopped by the Ryan home. Though she was no longer able to see Alina more than once every few months, she was still quick to respond to the Ryans' calls or emails, and she made time immediately after Julie had explained the previous day's events.

"Alina's been part of your family now for . . . five years, right?" Carol asked Julie.

They sat at the kitchen table, sipping coffee. All Julie could do was nod. She was utterly drained—of energy, of optimism, of hope. "Five years. I thought things would be so different at this point. But I can't be with her twenty-four hours a day, working to prevent her rages, and I can't spend hours of my day trying to calm her down once she's in them. Carol, this is tearing me apart. It's already torn my family apart." Julie took a deep breath. "Mark and I—we fight constantly. I think back on how we used to be, and it's like remembering two other people. I don't even feel married anymore."

"I've heard that before," Carol sympathized. "That's unfortunately a common story for parents of complex children with special needs. Have you two gone through any therapy, either individually or as a couple?"

Julie half-laughed. "In all of our spare time?"

"I'm telling you this as a support for the family and as a friend," Carol said. "Make the time. At least join a support group for parents of kids with reactive attachment disorder. And strongly consider marriage counseling. This is a cycle I've seen before. It can be broken, but you have to put in the effort."

Julie slumped in her seat, feeling entirely defeated.

"Look," Carol said, "you've done a remarkable job on your own and with the resources you've found for Alina. But we're at a point now where we may have to consider some alternatives."

"I feel like we've explored everything. I'm constantly on the Internet trying to find more ideas. What do you mean by 'other alternatives?'"

"There has been a long-standing pattern of extreme emotional and behavioral problems in the home. And now the home environment is clearly unsafe if Alina is pulling out knives and threatening to use them," Carol said bluntly. She held a hand out to stop Julie from interrupting. "She's also reaching a crucial point in her education with the transition to middle school coming up. That's big for any kid but huge for Alina. I don't think she's emotionally, behaviorally, or socially ready for that kind of change. All of this, plus what happened last night, cements it for me."

"Cements what?" Julie's hackles were rising, ready to protect her daughter if yet another person suggested Alina should be "returned."

"My thinking is that she needs more help and support than what can be provided right now at home." Carol reached for the leather bag sitting beside her on the cushioned bench. She pulled out a brochure and passed it across the table to Julie. "I'd like you and Mark to read this information. This is Genesee Lake School," she said. "It's near your home, close enough for you to visit every weekend, and it provides residential therapeutic and special education services for children, youth, and young adults with disabilities."

"Wait. You're suggesting that we put Alina in some kind of a . . . *home?*" Julie's voice rose indignantly. "Carol, I thought you, of all people—"

"Julie," Carol said, smiling gently. "I'm not suggesting that you abandon Alina. I'm not saying you should put her into another type of orphanage. What I'm recommending is that we keep following the paths we've been pursuing—seeking specialized help for your daughter—but her needs require more focused therapeutic supports and a higher level of care right now. Not forever, though. Everyone knows it's best for children to be at home with their families. However, sometimes their needs cannot be met at home or by the public school district, and they would benefit from short-term residential placement. Children go to residential therapeutic schools like Genesee Lake School to learn skills that will allow them to successfully return to their homes—and stay there. These schools also teach parents skills to understand their child's disability in a more supportive manner."

Julie ran a finger across the brochure's cover but didn't open it. "I don't know. This is all a lot to take in right now. Maybe we should just—"

"Look," Carol said, "let's be honest with each other here. You're not going to be able to do this for much longer."

"I—" Julie stopped. She stared into her coffee cup, feeling a moment of mortification when she noticed the flecks of cream that had risen to the top; the cream had expired. Great: the cream had expired, who knew when Luke would come home from school, Margaret was stationed in front of the television, and Mark had taken off work (again) to be with Alina in the psychiatric hospital. What thread of normalcy they were attempting to cling to was quickly unraveling. Where would they be in another year? Another five?

"I wouldn't make this recommendation if I didn't already have experience with this residential school," Carol said, "or if I thought there were a way for Alina to stay at home right now and keep you all a healthy, happy family—which is the goal, by the way." Carol smiled, and Julie offered a weak one in return. "Right now, it looks like it is time to try something different to eventually accomplish that goal."

Numbly, Julie nodded.

"Take a look at the brochure, talk to your husband, and spend some time on the school's website. If you'd like, give me a call Monday and I can set up a tour. We'll just see how you feel after that. Do you know when you're going to pick Alina up from the hospital?"

"Tomorrow," Julie whispered, hating the feeling of dread that rose to her throat.

"That gives you today to spend time with your other children, take a long bath, and start thinking about this possibility," Carol said. "If you have questions, call me any time."

Julie spent the rest of that afternoon doing online research. According to its website, Genesee Lake School pursued one major goal: to provide kids with social, emotional, and behavioral needs—the skills they need to return successfully to their home, school, and community. The school helped kids like Alina, as well as those with autism spectrum disorders, including Asperger's disorder, and mental retardation, depression, anxiety, traumatic brain injury, and a variety of other conditions. One second, Julie felt certain that Genesee Lake School was the right place for Alina, and the next she was thinking, *How is she going to get better if she's surrounded by other disabled kids?* She eventually slammed her laptop shut, warmed the water for another shower, and cried in peace.

By the time Mark got home, Julie's face was splotchy but composed. After dinner, she shared with him everything she'd researched, as well as the brochure Carol had given her, and she recounted their conversation.

"She offered to call Genesee Lake School for us and set up a tour," Julie said. "She also said it's just a tour—no commitment, and nothing is set in stone."

Mark sighed, washing the last dish and placing it in the dish rack to dry. "Residential treatment facilities. Who ever thought we'd adopt a child and bring her all the way from Russia, only to send her to live somewhere else? Ridiculous."

Julie was stricken. "Is that how you see this?"

Mark shook his head. "All I know, Julie, is that I am a damn tired man."

Julie stared at him for a moment before leaning on the counter, head in her hands. "I'm going to tell Carol to make the call to Genesee Lake School," she said, voice muffled. "At this point, we have nothing to lose and everything to gain."

CHAPTER 19
A STEP TOWARD HOPE

Once Alina was back in school the following week, Julie and Mark made the forty-five-minute drive from Milwaukee to Oconomowoc, Wisconsin, to visit Genesee Lake School. Susan, the admissions coordinator, had been friendly, warm, and patient with them on the phone, answering all their questions and sending them information about the therapeutic residential school program by overnight delivery. From everything Julie and Mark read in the information packet, as well as online—and what they'd already heard from Carol—Genesee Lake School sounded like it might be exactly what they needed: somewhere for Alina to get the kind of expertise, therapeutic supports, special education, medical care, dietary services, and overall quality care that they weren't able to provide right now at home. Somewhere staffed with people who understood children with attachment issues, who had worked with many kids like Alina, who worked together in an integrated and comprehensive manner all under one roof. People who also knew how to help her learn skills and grow despite the challenges that came with her disability. It all sounded great, Julie thought.

Now they just needed to see this kind of environment with their own eyes.

It was a Tuesday morning in early October, and Julie and Mark were mostly silent as they drove to Genesee Lake School. Mark had the radio on low, tuned to a soft rock station that faded into the background as Julie watched the trees blur past—smooth green lines punctuated by startling bursts of scarlet and marigold, like paint flicked from a brush and landing randomly on the canvas. When Mark pulled off I-94 and onto a side road, the street narrowed to two lanes and the spaces between trees widened to allow for modest one-story homes.

"Where are we?" Julie murmured as they drove farther from the highway.

Mark glanced at his iPhone. "This says we're going the right way."

They passed a small lake that shimmered with sunlight, and then came the sign for Genesee Lake School. Julie exhaled, relieved.

"Those must be some of the group homes," Mark said, gesturing to his right. "One is for kids and the other is for young adults. I read that they also have three in the middle of the community nearby."

Julie nodded, craning her neck as they passed three group homes that, according to the literature, both lower- and higher-skilled kids were able to live in as a transition point between the residential care and their own home. *If Alina does come to Genesee Lake School, maybe one day she'll be able to make that move as well,* Julie dared to hope.

They pulled into the parking lot and then walked hand in hand to the school. Though she had seen pictures, Julie was pleasantly surprised by how open and airy the entrance hall was. The floors were shiny concrete, stained a rust-color with interludes of green that reminded her of patches of grass. Stone pillars led to a high ceiling bordered with windows. Below each rectangular window was what looked like a blackboard of the same dimensions, and each blackboard showed a different quote:

The future belongs to those who believe in the beauty of their dreams. —ELEANOR ROOSEVELT.

I am still learning. —MICHAELANGELO.

And one that resonated with Julie: *A journey of a thousand miles must start with a single step.* —LAO TZU.

Is this a single step? she thought.

"This feels nice," Julie said, inexplicably feeling the need to whisper.

Mark nodded. "Let's go sign in."

At a window to their right, they were greeted and given name tags by a nice lady named Laurie. They milled around for only a minute or two before Susan, the admissions coordinator they'd spoken with on the phone, joined them in the lobby.

"Mr. and Mrs. Ryan," she said, smiling, "it's so nice to meet you in person."

Susan was in her thirties, with a blond bob and alert blue eyes. She exuded a genuine, friendly energy that immediately put Julie at ease.

"Well, we're happy to be here," Julie said. Mark cast her a sidelong glance, and Julie amended quietly, "Well, 'happy' may not be the best choice of words."

Susan smiled. "I know what you meant. If you both are ready, I'd love to show you around. I'll tell you about our school, but if you have any questions, please feel free to ask."

For the next hour, Susan walked Julie and Mark around both floors of Genesee Lake School. Julie took photos with her phone so that she'd remember the details later: the cobalt blue lockers that were made of plastic to minimize the loud banging that overwhelmed so many of the students; the wider hallways, which gave students a more comfortable berth and minimized incidents of accidental bumping; the sweet crepe paper murals with cut-out autumn leaves that said *Falling Into School*.

If the hallways were the school's arms and legs, the classrooms were its arteries. Susan led them into two or three different classes, where they stood in the back of the room and quietly watched for five or ten minutes at a time. It was like no school that Julie and Mark had ever seen before. While each class had "normal" desks—either individual ones or tables—they also had some that looked like college library carrels, others that were at standing height, and some with large rubber therapy balls tucked beneath them instead of chairs. There were ten students or fewer per class, supported by one teacher, one teacher aide, and two additional support staff for those children who needed extra assistance. Each class had a written or visual schedule on either the dry erase board or the walls, which Susan said was extremely helpful to the kids, who were often stronger as visual learners. The classrooms also had other educational and therapeutic supports posted on the walls, such as a poster demonstrating the requirements for "respectful listening": *eye to eye contact*, with a drawing of two silhouetted faces, an arrow connecting one set of eyes to the other; *wait your turn*, with an illustration of a hand held palm out; *sit still at your desk*, with a photo of a smiling girl with her chin cupped in her hands; *listen with an open mind*, with a drawing of an ear with the word *listen* beside it; and *take a deep breath*, with a photo of a woman whose serene face was tipped toward the sun, the ocean in soft focus over her shoulder.

Susan then guided them toward the gym. Mark breathed deeply when they walked through the doors, smiling at Julie and remembering in a flash his younger years playing basketball. The gym was all gleaming wood floors, with one basketball hoop on either end. Three staff members worked with three kids on the floor, while two other students sat with their backs against the cinderblock walls. One wore a dark beanie pulled low over his forehead, while earbuds dangled from another girl's ears.

"Those types of things—the hat and earbuds—wouldn't be allowed in a public school gym," Julie observed quietly, nodding toward the two students.

Susan nodded. "Up until a few years ago, they weren't allowed here, either," she said. "But these kids are already pretty rigid thinkers, and when we meet their rigidity with our own—well, let's just say they don't cancel each other out," she said, smiling. "Plus, with the collaborative problem-solving approach we use, adults tend to care about kids' behaviors if they fall under health, learning, safety, or impact of behavior on others. If they don't fall under one of these categories—which the hat and earbuds don't—we have to ask ourselves why we care in the first place and adjust our expectations accordingly."

Julie and Mark exchanged glances. *Health, learning, safety, impact of behavior on others . . . expectations.* They thought about what Susan said about inflexibility and rigidity. They had tried being inflexible in their expectations with Alina. They had always thought that negative behavior should be followed by strong negative consequences, even if they were presented with paternal love, so Alina had lost privileges and toys at home and points and stickers in school; that was what some of the therapists had told them to do. Already, this early in the tour, they were wondering how poorly equipped they had been to expect to raise Alina successfully with her current level of need—a thought that ballooned in Julie's chest with a sense of guilt and failure.

"Why don't we go check out the indoor sensory playground," Susan said, as if sensing Julie and Mark's emotions.

The Ryans followed Susan down the hallway to a room resembling a smaller gym, with two swings hanging from the ceiling low to the ground. The seats were upholstered and wide enough for a child to sprawl across, and bright padding against the wall ensured low, harmless impact. In a corner, plastic padded mats—similar to those used in gymnastics—were stacked up so that children could climb and jump on them.

"We bring students here a couple of times a day so they can use the room to help self-regulate. Once they are regulated, they are more available for learning. Plus, we know it helps to get kids out of the classroom to get some exercise and let off some steam," Susan explained. "We also use the swings and activities in this room to expand and elaborate upon social interactions, engagement, and relating with others."

"How does that work?" Mark asked.

"Let's talk about the swings, for example." Susan walked

toward a swing, pulling it slightly toward her and releasing. "If we've seen that a child enjoys the swing, we take their lead, harness that natural interest, in order to encourage her to express herself in gestures or words—let us know whether she wants to go faster or slower, keep going or to stop. This is good work on relating, communicating, and thinking, all through an interaction surrounding her own natural interest. We find that when we are more interactive, responsive, and collaborative with the students, we see happier kids with less behavior problems."

Julie nodded. "That sounds great, Susan, but there always seems to be a point of no return with Alina," she said. "Once she hits a certain level, the rage goes on for hours."

"I know," Susan said. "A lot of our kids are like that, especially when they first arrive here. We work with our staff on understanding each child's cycle of escalation. In relatively straightforward terms, that's their pattern of rumbling, rage, and recovery. If you can catch a child during the rumbling stage, when you realize there has been some kind of trigger and you start seeing, for example, pacing, louder voice, facial flushing, maybe a certain kind of look, then she's starting to become upset but is still rational. This is the time to intervene. Once children are in rage, rationality is lacking and our best approach is just to give them space and support to enhance emotional and behavioral de-arousal and self-control. Physical intervention may be necessary if their behavior presents imminent danger to themselves or others, but we teach the kids to use their 'tools'—or coping and problem-solving strategies—when they are in the rumbling stage prior to rage. With some kids, maybe like

Alina, it can be tough to engage that thinking process during times of high emotion, and we have found that more sensory-based strategies—and a focus on repetitive, rhythmic, and body-based activities—" Susan let go of the swing, "is helpful."

Julie felt a strong mix of emotions as they left the sensory playground. She was trying to remain centered, but her first feeling was utter frustration—why hadn't someone told them these things sooner? She wondered what their home life could have been like if they had focused more on sensory regulation strategies and less on the rigidity of their own interactions with Alina. How different could things have been if they had paid more attention to Alina's escalation cues in order to prevent her rage reactions? The second, and more conflicting feeling, was relief—a sense of wary optimism. Maybe it *was* possible for Alina to show improvement, learn more social and emotional skills, have more independence, and—as much as possible—live a normal life. Maybe it came down to all of them—Mark and Julie, the entire family, the school, everyone who came into meaningful contact with Alina—to use some of the methods Susan had shared with them. Julie's mind was in a flurry of "maybes" and "possibilities" as they walked toward the dorms.

"Since the kids are in school right now," Susan said, "I'll show you the dorms, which have group living, bedroom, and bathroom areas."

They turned a corner and were greeted with a spacious, cheerfully painted room. One wall was fuschia, the other lime green, and cut-out paper butterflies decorated the sides of the fluorescent lights. Wood and leather chairs were grouped throughout the room, each bearing a girl's name taped on laminated construction paper to the base. There were paintings on the walls and sheer polka-dotted curtains over the windows, with shelving at the back wall filled with books and board games. A large-screen TV sat at the front of the room. Julie couldn't help but smile. It reminded her of her freshman dorm common area.

"As you can see, this is obviously a girls' dorm," Susan said, smiling. "This is their group living area, mostly for recreation and leisure, where they often spend time after school, during free time, and before they go to bed."

Susan led them down the hall, opening up several doors to show them the rooms. Each was a uniform size, large enough to fit a twin bed, a chest of drawers, and a desk. Some girls had magazine cutouts and drawings on the walls, and others displayed family photos and movie posters. The bedding was different in each room, clearly brought from home, and again Julie was reminded of a cheerful college dorm, where girls might lay on each other's beds and gossip about boys. She didn't know if anything like that went on here, but the atmosphere was one that felt conducive to that sort of positivity—that kind of normalcy.

"This is nice," Mark said as they walked. "I don't know what I expected, but I don't think it was this."

"I agree," Julie said.

Susan smiled. "This is a new environment, and we want the kids to feel as comfortable and safe here as possible."

Julie nodded but suddenly felt short of breath. As comforted as she was by Susan and the tour, it hit her again forcefully that if they made the choice that seemed inevitable, soon Alina would be living here and *not* at home. It was difficult to fight the belief that she was giving up on her daughter and their capacity to care for her. It took great effort to try to look at things in a more helpful and accurate manner and to tell herself, *This is the exact opposite of giving up. This is giving her what she needs and what we need.*

"Thank you for taking so much time with us today," Julie said once they were back at the front entrance.

"It's truly been my pleasure," Susan replied. "Do you have any questions? I know this is a lot for you to think about."

Mark glanced at Julie. "Well, we obviously need to talk," he said, "but I think we're both impressed by Genesee Lake School and what it has to offer our daughter."

Julie nodded.

"After we talk, and assuming we want to move forward, what are the next steps?" Mark asked.

"Well, there are some logistics," Susan said. "Carol mentioned on the phone that she's working with you to secure funding from the state for Alina's placement. That means you'll have to file a non-violent CHIPS petition."

"What's that?" Julie asked, pulling out her ubiquitous notebook.

"CHIPS stands for Child In Need of Protective Services," Susan explained. "In most cases, this is a petition an attorney files against parents or caregivers who are suspected of abuse. In your case, you are filing *as* her parents, and you'll file a non-violent petition, which basically says you're *temporarily* giving up your rights to have Alina live in your home in order for her to receive protective services."

The first tendrils of panic coiled around Julie's heart. "Giving up our rights? Our parental rights? I didn't know anything about this. I—" She trailed off, looking back and forth between Mark and Susan, imagining the desperation they must be seeing in her face.

"No, you're not giving up your parental rights," Susan said, her voice low and soothing. "You're still Alina's parents and will be the ones who give informed consent for any kind of medication, treatment, or therapy that she receives at Genesee Lake School. And remember, this is a temporary situation. It's just part of the red tape that parents unfortunately have to go through to secure funding. If you decide to have Alina referred to Genesee Lake School, Carol will make sure that a county social worker is assigned to help you through the process."

"And how should we tell Alina about all this?" Julie's throat tightened. "I don't have the slightest clue how to tell her she won't be living with us anymore."

"That's not an easy thing for any parent. Big change is hard for all of us and more so for children with special needs," Susan said. "The best advice we give parents is to communicate the news in a developmentally appropriate and supportive manner, and to frame it in realistic terms. Let her know this is not forever, none of this is her fault, and that you will talk, visit, and bring her home for visits. Let her know it is an opportunity to learn new skills, like when she learned to tie her shoes for the first time and how that got a lot easier, so that things will go better when she returns home all the time with your family. I would tell her that this is a special school that you are excited to have her come to so that she can learn new things. I would show her some pictures of Genesee Lake

School—the website, any photos you've taken today—and then we could schedule a few tours or visits with Alina. If you decide to pursue placement, and funding is not an issue with the county—and right now it sounds positive—we're probably at least four weeks out from placement, so we should use that time wisely to help with her adjustment."

Julie nodded. "That's good advice and guidance," she said. "Thank you so much for all your help, Susan."

Susan smiled and reached forward to shake both of their hands. "Of course. Call me if you have any questions or need more information," she said. "We look forward to hearing from you both and from Carol on your decision. Once a referral is made, our admissions team will review it carefully."

"Admissions team? How much time will that take?" asked Julie, suddenly not feeling so optimistic.

"We meet weekly and could review Alina's case soon, maybe as early as next week if funding is at least tentatively secured."

"Okay," Julie said, sighing in relief. "Thank you again."

"Of course," said Susan. "There is one more thing I want to tell you, though," she said, smiling.

"What's that?" Mark asked.

"Just this." Susan looked directly at both of them, a kind smile still on her face. "Times right now seem tough—but remember, there's always hope."

CHAPTER 20
I ALREADY HAVE A SCHOOL

Strange things. Strange things were happening. Mama and Papa were talking to Alina about a special school.

"In a few years, Luke is going to go away for school, too," Mama said. "It's an exciting time where he'll make new friends and learn a lot—but he doesn't get to go for three more years. You get to go now. Doesn't that sound just super?"

"No," Alina said. In Mama's lap, wrapped in a blanket, Mama rocking. "I don't want the special school. I want to stay home."

"How about we look at some pictures?"

Alina liked pictures. Liked drawing and coloring, too.

Mama shifted, one arm around Alina and other arm showing Alina papers. "Look at these pictures. Aren't they neat?" Mama flipped pages. Kissed Alina's head. "And look at the pictures of the woods—all the trees and grass. You love trees and grass. Don't you think you could have fun there?"

Alina ran her fingers over the trees. She liked trees. Liked grass and insects, but Mama said no insects in pockets. She liked wings. Wings that sparkled in the sun.

Butterfly wings that left dust on her fingers. Hard wings and soft wings.

"Alina? What do you think?"

"Pretty," Alina said softly.

"See, the special school is right next to these woods. Your teachers and staff will take you outside to play."

"I still don't want to go," Alina said. "I want to stay home."

"Remember, you'll come back home on weekends." Mama kissed Alina's head. "You'll only sleep there during the week. And while you're there, you'll have lots of fun in school, and you'll learn all sorts of new things."

"I already have a school."

"I know, honey, but remember, this one is a special school. We'll go visit Genesee Lake School soon so you can see."

Alina and her parents then visited the special school. Alina looked at everything and everyone. It was different from her school, with Ms. Natalie, Mrs. Rodriguez, and this year, Mrs. Jackson.

"Where's Mrs. Jackson?" Alina asked. "She'll come here, too?"

"No, honey," Mama said. "But we can go back and visit her. Remember, like how we used to visit Ms. Natalie when you were little?"

"Ms. Natalie." Alina remembered her.

More visits. Then a "courtroom." Alina sat next to a man. A stranger. Alina heard Mama say that he was a "guardian *ad litem*." People talked a lot. The room was cold and brown. Mama and Papa stood, spoke, sat, and looked nervous. They looked at Alina, looked at each other, held hands in their laps. Alina sat quietly, watching and listening. After a while, Alina started to feel scared. Mama said courtroom had to happen before special school, but Alina didn't want either. Alina just wanted to go home.

Luke, at home. Luke didn't talk to Alina much. But Luke said, "Are you excited about going to this new school?"

Alina shook her head. "No." Luke was chewing gum. "Can I have some gum?"

Luke pulled a green pack from his pocket. Unwrapped a stick and handed it to Alina. Alina smiled at him and stuffed the gum into her mouth.

Margaret, in a blanket. "Alina's leaving?"

"She's going away to a school where you also live," Luke said. "But not forever."

Margaret was quiet. Sucked on the edge of the blanket. Alina stared at her until she looked away.

"I don't want to," Alina said. "I want to stay here."

"Don't worry," Luke said. Nice voice. "I bet you'll like it."

CHAPTER 21
IT TAKES A VILLAGE

Several weeks after their appearance in court, Julie and Mark drove Alina back up to Genesee Lake School. Two large suitcases bumped each other in the back of the SUV—one with Alina's clothes and the other with her sheets and comforter. They had taken her shopping to pick out something she liked, hoping it would give her a feeling of power and control, and she had chosen purple jersey sheets with a fuchsia bed cover. She was mostly quiet for the drive, occasionally reminding them that she didn't want to go to the special school. Each time Alina issued a protest, Julie had to take a deep breath to keep from crying. She felt like they were signing their daughter away.

Inside, they met with Melanie, Alina's clinical coordinator, and Samantha, the residential group supervisor. Melanie was in her mid-thirties, with a bright smile and reassuring manner. She would be Julie and Mark's main point of contact throughout Alina's stay at the Genesee Lake School and would offer individual therapy and family sessions. Samantha was in her late twenties, tall and sturdy with minimal makeup and brown hair clipped at the nape of her neck. She wore khaki slacks and a polo shirt, and she introduced herself warmly to Alina.

"Alina, your mom and dad said you brought some things from home," Samantha said. "How about we go get your room arranged and decorated, just how you like it?"

Alina looked tiny and fragile in this room of adults, her eyes flitting between them. She didn't respond, and Julie cringed. Passive noncompliance. *Here it comes,* Julie thought, but she said instead, "I think that sounds like a great idea. Alina, you can show Samantha the sheets and comforter we bought, and you can also hang up your pictures."

At the word *pictures*, Alina's blue-gray eyes brightened. A corner of her mouth hooked into a faint semblance of a smile, and after another minute, Alina followed Samantha out of the room.

Julie sighed with relief, looking at Mark. "I didn't think she was going to do it."

"Neither did I."

"It's a positive start," Melanie said, smiling. "Why don't we sit down? Would you two like some coffee?"

"That's okay," Julie said.

Mark shook his head. "We practically robbed a Starbucks on the way over."

Melanie laughed, and all three took seats at a round wooden table. "So, since you've already completed most of the admissions packet," she said, referring to a previous visit, "what I'd like to do now is talk about what the next few months will look like. Is that all right with you both?"

Julie nodded, recalling going through the thick sheaf of paperwork and signing her name so many times her hand cramped.

Seeming to read Julie's mind, Melanie said, "I know you've gone through a lot to be here now. Not just with Alina's behavior but with the county, school, court, funding—all those things. Going to court, I'm sure, was probably quite difficult."

Julie bit her lip. "A part of me still worries there's some trick and that we actually *have* given up our rights and guardianship of Alina."

Melanie smiled. "That's not the first time I've heard that. But you are still absolutely Alina's parents. We can't initiate any treatment, including medical care, medication, or therapy, without your written consent, which you can revoke at any time. Okay?"

Julie exhaled. "Okay."

"Also," Melanie said, "you will be involved in goal setting for all of Alina's treatment at Genesee Lake School. As her parents, you're an integral part of her treatment."

Julie's leg was pulsing beneath the table, rocking the surface. She didn't notice until Mark put a familiar hand on her knee.

Melanie leaned across the table and looked her in the eyes. "It's difficult, but you're doing the right thing for Alina and your family."

Julie nodded. "I know."

After a few more minutes, in which Julie and Mark answered more questions about Alina's history, interests, and personal strengths and challenges, Melanie said, "Remember—no one stays here forever. Our goal with all the kids is to teach them skills that will allow them to successfully return to their home, school, and community. We want Alina to eventually become more independent and move to a less restrictive environment, whether that means living in one of our group homes for a while or returning permanently to your home and family."

"How will you know when she's ready for that kind of transition?" Mark asked. "What kind of therapy will she receive here? She can be so aggressive and distrustful of others that I can't imagine how long it'll take her to actually open up to whatever you all do here."

You're the one who's aggressive, Julie wanted to snap at her husband, but she bit her tongue the way she usually did, knowing this was difficult for him, too.

Melanie smiled understandingly. "We believe that everybody wants to do well in life. You, me, and also the kids. We believe that *kids do well if they can* . . . and if they can't, we adults have to figure out why so we can help. This is the philosophy of the Think:Kids Collaborative Problem Solving approach, and we believe it one hundred percent. In the case of Alina, as well as other kids with a history of ongoing and chronic behavior problems, although behavior can seem manipulative, intentional, and goal directed, this is not usually the case. According to collaborative problem solving, ongoing and chronic behavioral problems are a form of learning disability, the byproduct of underdeveloped critical thinking skills necessary for flexibility, frustration tolerance, and problem solving. Within a month of her admission, Alina's treatment team will meet to assess areas of skill weakness and strength so that we can get a better idea of what is preventing more socially adaptive behavior.

"Also, given your daughter's early experiences," continued Melanie, "her version of self, others, and the world has been skewed in a negative direction. That perspective can be changed through therapeutic connections and relationships over time. I believe that a huge benefit of a residential therapeutic program like Genessee Lake School is having all of the therapeutic, educational, and medical services and supports in one integrated setting. That allows an opportunity for kids like Alina to rework some of those connections and beliefs and also feel a sense of hope and optimism toward the future and their place in the world. Mark," Melanie said conversationally, "how do you think Alina perceives herself, others, and the world?"

Mark blinked. "I have no idea. What do you think?" he asked, lobbing the question back at Melanie.

Melanie smiled. "It's hard to tell right now. Not only have I not spent enough time with her, but Alina hasn't been able to express to you what she is thinking and feeling. Still, *behavior is a form of communication*. A child may not be able to use words well, but by looking at their behavior closely, we can often make some good guesses as to what they may be trying to communicate or express."

"Whatever the case may be, it sounds like changing her perceptions of self, others, and the world is a big part of the goal?" Julie asked, looking up.

"Exactly," Melanie said.

"How do you do that?" Mark asked.

"We follow trauma-informed care principles and practices as an organization," Melanie said. "Trauma-informed care represents a mindset shift in which we stop asking what is wrong with the child and start asking what happened to her. We want to recognize the impact of trauma on kids in all areas, but we prioritize safety, choice, collaboration, skill building, and healing relationships. It's a big job, as you know, so we increase our caregiver capacity by taking care of our staff."

Julie hadn't thought about the last part. "Your staff must also feel the effects of working with kids who have histories of extreme stress."

Melanie nodded. "Definitely. Our direct care staff are the true heroes of the organization. We need to make sure their needs are met so they can continue doing the same for our kids."

"Kind of how we need to take of ourselves in order to be the best parents we can be," Julie said.

"Which is exactly what we haven't done lately," Mark added.

Melanie let Mark's last statement sit for a moment, and Julie appreciated the space. Then Melanie said quietly, "Prioritizing your own needs as individuals and as a couple probably hasn't seemed nearly as important as keeping Alina and the rest of your family safe."

Julie looked away, willing the sudden sting in her eyes to abate. She let out her breath shakily. "No," she said. "It hasn't seemed as important. It hasn't even been *possible*."

Melanie nodded. "You know," she said, "what you two have been through in the last few years could have flattened you. But as exhausted as you are, as much as you feel you could have done better—because good parents always feel they could have done better," she added with a smile, "you have not given up. That you're sitting here is proof of that. Just for a moment, let yourselves feel proud of that."

Julie looked down at her lap. There was her binder, stuffed with pages indented with her neatly slanted writing, and there were her hands, dry and tense. She stared at her wedding band. She and Mark may not be the easy, intimate couple they used to be, but they were together. They were partners, teammates, throughout this whole ordeal, and Julie smiled as she felt a wash of tenderness for her husband.

"What?" Mark asked softly.

Julie startled. She hadn't realized he was looking at her. "I'm just feeling proud of us," she said softly.

Mark's face softened, and he reached for her hand. Julie let herself simply enjoy the familiar feel of his fingers sliding between hers. She smiled at him, and he smiled back. Finally, they returned their attention to Melanie.

"Thank you for that," Mark said, clearing his throat. "So . . . you were saying. Trauma-informed care?"

Melanie smiled. "Yes. In trauma-informed care, children and families are viewed as experts on their lives. We know that healing happens in healthy relationships, and symptoms are viewed as adaptations—not something to decrease or cover up. The focus is on supportive, relationship-based interventions.

"I mentioned that it takes an organization-wide effort," Melanie continued, "and I meant it. Trauma-informed care involves kids, parents, families, stakeholders, funders, and all employees—from housekeeping to executive leadership—to foster growth in our kids. Yes, kids should ideally be at home with their families, but if their needs require short-term residential placement, then it's important that everyone work together. It truly does take a village to raise a child, whether that's at home or at Genesee Lake School."

"I guess so," Julie said, looking at Mark. "And we've

been trying so desperately to do it on our own."

"You've done everything you could," Melanie said reassuringly. She turned to Mark. "And to continue answering your earlier question about therapy, Alina and I will have individual psychotherapy sessions each week. Once she and I establish a working therapeutic relationship, we'll strive toward additional goals like problem-solving skills, emotion management or coping skills, and real life behavioral exercises. She'll also participate in weekly group therapy with several other girls. They'll learn about mindfulness, distress tolerance, and interpersonal and coping skills."

"That sounds intense," Mark commented.

Melanie smiled. "We try to make the group fun and engaging. Kids learn better that way. Of course, Alina will also participate in our special education program, with community and skill-building therapeutic activities built into the school day. There will be opportunities to learn relaxation skills, social skills, and communication and regulation strategies, as well as to work within an adapted and enriched academic curriculum."

"It sounds like exactly what she needs," Julie said.

"The services I've talked about are important, no doubt," Melanie said, "but you know, I think the most important factor for kids in our program is just daily life. We call it a 'therapeutic milieu'—the day-to-day experiences from the time the kids wake till the time they go to bed. It's the positive and supportive interactions, connections, and relationships with peers and adults that really build that sense of certainty, sensitivity, structure, and routine—things that all kids need but especially those with challenges such as Alina's. Through multiple intervention points, we're able to teach kids important life and thinking skills so that they can achieve more independence and growth. Ultimately, through everything we do, we want to provide Alina with a sense of personal control and hope for the future."

As Julie listened, it struck her that as powerless as she'd felt in the years since bringing Alina home, her daughter had probably felt powerless her entire life—completely at the mercy of others' moods, demands, expectations, behavior, and desires. She remembered Dr. Brook's words: she and Mark were not just Alina's parents. They were her advocates; her champions. They had to be.

"Another point I want to make," Melanie said, "is that it isn't just Alina's worldview that we want to change. A lot of times, adults need to reconstruct their views of the child."

Instinctively, Julie's eyebrows drew together over her nose, and she forced herself to relax her defensive expression. "What do you mean?"

"It's natural for us to create explanations for certain behaviors," Melanie said. "If Alina rages when you tell her *no*, for example, you might think she's trying to control you. Naturally, as parents, you'd want her to know you're in control, and you might lean toward issuing negative consequences. But it's important for all of us—including the staff here—to remember the impact of poor attachment and interpersonal trauma on brain development and social and cognitive development," Melanie said.

"We know it's not her fault, if that's what you mean," Mark said. "We recognized that a long time ago."

Melanie nodded. "That's good. But like I said before,

behavior is a form of communication. The question we should ask when she demonstrates challenging behavior is: what is she communicating? We've worked a great deal over the past few years with Dr. Stuart Ablon from Think:Kids in Boston, and he always tells us to remember that 'your explanation guides your intervention.' In other words, how we make sense out of behavior, or anything in life, will guide how we respond to it. If our explanation is that the behavior is purposeful or intentional, such as seeking attention, then our intervention will be to use consequences such as planned ignoring to decrease the behavior. But if our explanation for the behavior is that she has underdeveloped skills necessary for flexibility, frustration tolerance, and problem solving, our intervention will be to teach her problem-solving skills through therapeutic relationships with adults so that she can use these skills in the future. This shift in mindset is huge for parents and anyone working with kids who demonstrate consistent challenging behavior."

Julie's mind was racing. The concept was so simple and made so much sense. She realized she could apply that perspective shift to Mark and Luke and many others in her life. Or who used to be in her life, she corrected herself, thinking of the friends who had dropped off, seemingly with disinterest, over the years. Julie was surprised by the flicker of excitement she felt at the idea of practicing this line of thought.

"For problem solving," Melanie said, "we teach our kids about 'thinking things through.' What is the problem here? What is my goal? What are my options or choices? What are the consequences of each? Which one looks best? How can I practice this? Also, for emotions, what are the emotions I feel? How does my body feel? What do I think when I feel these emotions? How can I express them best? What can others do, and what can I do to help myself during difficult emotional situations? What are my tools to fix negative emotions?"

Julie and Mark exchanged glances. "That's not exactly how her mind works . . ." Julie said.

"She might not be able to handle all of that—but we try to meet every child where he or she is at to build upon skills over time. So if she isn't able to process all the questions I asked, we will find out where she is in problem solving and emotion regulation and build on it over time."

Social problem solving, emotion management, and stress reduction and coping skills would be primary parts of the planned therapeutic environment, Melanie explained. For example, one goal would be to have Alina eventually react more thoughtfully and assertively rather than impulsively and aggressively.

"This helps to rework her sense of self," Melanie said. "If we can help Alina understand that she has mastery over herself and influence over her environment, then her behavior will change accordingly."

"What about when she does rage?" Mark asked. "Because, as good as this all sounds, she *will* rage. How do you deal with that?"

"It's crucial for Alina to recognize over time that the power lies within her and not exclusively within the adults; that's why hierarchical responses like punishment or removal of privileges aren't helpful for relational repair," Melanie answered. "Instead, we work in partnership with the child and pay attention to triggers. We focus on supportive de-escalation and building self-awareness through self-calming tools and coping strategies. Then, when she is calm, we can communicate and teach thinking skills through collaborative problem solving.

"Again," Melanie said, "it's about relational repair. We also rely on our occupational therapists for sensory-based interventions to help kids regulate emotions and behavior, as well as modulate arousal—so we have 'calming rooms' instead of 'time-out rooms.' These are now safe havens with sensory-based strategies instead of kids being sent for an adult-dictated amount of time to a silent, empty room. A major part of trauma-informed care is that we want to avoid coercive or forceful practices with kids, because the relationship is the vehicle toward change."

"The relationship is the vehicle toward change," Julie murmured, scribbling another note. She had found it helpful lately to adopt short mantras she could repeat to herself in times of stress with Alina. This one had a soothing, positive, optimistic quality that Julie appreciated. Others she'd noted throughout the conversation were "Kids do well if they can," "Behavior is a form of communication," "Your explanation guides your intervention," "Respect, responsibility, and safety," and "It's never too late to strengthen developmental foundations in relating, communicating, and thinking."

"So when you say avoid coercive or forceful practices with kids," Mark said, "what does that mean, exactly?"

"Well, we don't want to retraumatize kids," Melanie explained, "so we minimize the use of physical restraint and seclusion—which is actually a national initiative and one we think is way overdue," she added. "Last, as far as the rages you mentioned, Mr. Ryan, prevention is key.

Once we work with her to recognize her triggers, we try to intervene *before* she reaches that painful, non-rational place of rage you both know so well. The most important thing we've learned is that when a kid is in rage, it is not the time to discipline, scold, teach right versus wrong, or often even talk. Talk when the child is calm, because she's not hearing you when she's that upset."

The longer they sat in Melanie's office, the more overwhelmed Julie felt. She was overwhelmed with information; overwhelmed with guilt because the more she heard, the more it seemed they had done wrong; and—finally, beautifully—overwhelmed with a sense of hope. Alina was in a place where she would be understood. Julie and Mark loved Alina, but they had never understood her, and now that she would be surrounded by people who did, maybe she could truly grow. Maybe the whole family could.

"This is a lot to process, I know," Melanie said, "but these conversations with you are going to be just as essential as our work with Alina. As her parents, it's crucial that you both have a strong understanding of her disability characteristics, her strengths and challenges, her treatment plan, and her transition planning. Youth-guided and family-driven care are major parts of our process at Genesee Lake School."

"It's definitely a lot to take in," Julie agreed, "and we obviously have a lot to learn, but it's all we want. How often should we come visit?"

"Once a week is ideal at the start," Melanie said. "It's important for her to know you love her and haven't abandoned her, because those might be her first thoughts. She'll probably want to talk to you on the phone a lot.

Feel free to call every night to let her know you're still supporting her. That will help with her adjustment."

"We can do that," Mark said, nodding.

"Thank you so much." Julie smiled first at Melanie and then at Mark, hoping he was feeling as optimistic as she was. He smiled back. The exhaustion, though, remained in his eyes.

"Unless you guys have any questions, why don't we go see how Alina and Samantha are doing?" Melanie asked.

Julie nodded, feeling as though they'd been at the table for hours. Melanie walked them through the residential area until they reached Alina's room. One wall was painted a glossy blue, the others white, and a window by the bed overlooked lush treed grounds. The bed was bright and cheerful with the bedclothes they had brought. Alina sat near the wall, staring outside with a neutral expression on her face.

"There are those woods we looked at in the pictures," Julie said, smiling. "Aren't they pretty?"

Alina didn't look at her, but she offered a slight nod.

Julie sat on the edge of the bed and patted the space beside her. After a brief hesitation, Alina scooted closer. "You and Samantha did a great job setting up your room, sweetie," Julie said. "It feels homey."

"This is not my home," Alina said.

"No," agreed Samantha, who was standing near the doorway. "Home is still home. But we can work together to make this *feel* like home."

"We're all here to support you," Melanie added. "Mom and Dad and I are going to talk to you on the phone every week, and anytime you want to call them, just let one of us know."

Julie and Mark lingered for a while longer, helping Alina tuck her clothing in drawers and tape photos to the walls before recognizing that they shouldn't delay leaving any longer.

"Honey," Julie said, extending an arm around Alina's shoulders. "It's time for Papa and I to leave. We'll be back to visit on Saturday, okay? In the meantime, you can call us any time you want, and we'll call tomorrow to see how you're doing."

Alina's shoulders were rigid, the bones still sharp beneath Julie's hands. When she finally looked at Julie, her eyes glinted in a way Julie had never seen. Alina was crying—with tears. In that moment, Julie almost took it all back, almost swept Alina into her arms and ran out, back to the car, back to their home and their lives. It took every ounce of strength for Julie to hug and kiss her daughter and step into the hallway while Mark did the same. She leaned against the wall, breathing deeply. That was when she noticed that the open wooden door of Alina's room already bore her name. It was scripted on bright pink laminated construction paper, and somehow it gave Julie the reassurance she needed to stay put, to not barrel back inside the room and take her daughter into her arms. It meant that it was her room—her place.

Mark had moved back into Alina's doorway.

"We love you, Alina," he said.

"I love you, too," Alina said quietly from inside her room.

"Samantha will help you keep settling in," Melanie said, "and I'll come back tomorrow morning to see how you're doing. How about I take you to school and introduce you to your teacher? That would be neat."

Julie listened carefully but didn't hear Alina reply. When Mark and Melanie emerged from her room, Mark's eyes glistened behind his glasses, and he swallowed repeatedly. Julie took his hand as Melanie walked them out of the residential school.

"I know that must have been hard for you," Melanie said, "but you did great during a difficult time. I'll call you tomorrow afternoon with an update on how Alina is doing. Of course, call me any time."

CHAPTER 22
SCARED

"Remember the group living area?" Samantha. "You came and saw it with your mom and dad when you visited. This is where the girls like to hang out after school and at night. They have some social groups, play games, read books, and watch TV. We also have movie nights and spa nights. Do you like movies?"

Alina stood next to Samantha, looking around. One wall bright pink. One wall bright green. Paper butterflies taped to the lights. "I like butterflies," Alina said quietly.

"Oh, yeah?" Samantha smiled. "What do you like about them?"

"Their colors. And wings."

"Well, we get lots of butterflies out here in the spring. We'll make sure we go outside and enjoy them. I heard you like to draw. How about drawing butterflies? Would you like that?"

Alina shrugged. "Maybe."

"Okay, well, that's something we can do together later." Samantha smiled. Samantha walked with Alina to a couple of armchairs. Alina sat down and Samantha did, too. "I know this is all new for you. How about we make it a little easier and go over our daily routine?"

Alina said nothing. Looked around. TV on, two girls watching. Laughter.

Samantha talked a lot. Said the kids woke up at seven, "completed their personal self-care and showers," ate breakfast at eight-fifteen, and went to school from nine to two forty-five. After school, different activities. "There are group outings and some fitness and exercise, and then there's free time before bed. That's when a lot of the girls hang out in here and spend time together."

Alina looked at girls watching TV. Giggling.

"We do have some expectations here. Check these out." Samantha pointed at words on wall: Respect, Responsibility, Safety. "This goes for all our kids—and the entire school staff as well. We should use respectful behavior and language toward each other, even when we're upset—which means no hitting, pushing, or swearing. For responsibility, we complete our personal self-care, go to school on time, and participate in school and group area activities. Safety is also important. We stay in the area we're supposed to be in and ask permission to leave if we need to. We don't want anyone wandering away, because that can be dangerous. How does all that sound? Any questions?"

Alina lowered and then lifted her head, looking directly at Samantha. "Call Mama and Papa."

"You want to call Mom and Dad right now."

Alina said yes.

Called home, but Mama and Papa sounded different. Far away. Alina was mostly quiet, but when Mama said, "I love you," Alina said, "I love you, too."

That night, weird dreams. Alina alone in a little white

room. No doors or windows. When she pushed against the walls, walls moved backwards. She pushed and pushed, and the walls moved back and back. Room got bigger, and Alina felt smaller. So much space around her but no one there. Still no doors or windows, still no noise, so Alina screamed in her dream. She was afraid. No one came.

Next day. Morning. Room getting brighter with sun. Knock on door. Alina didn't want to get up. World felt bad. Curled into wall when door opened.

"Good morning, Alina." Soft voice. Melanie. "Rise and shine. It's time to wake up."

Alina pulled blankets over her head. Only word in her brain was *no*. Didn't want to be here. Didn't know these people. Wanted to go home to *her* room, *her* bed, Mama and Papa.

"Alina, it's time to get out of bed and get dressed. Time to start your day."

Melanie kept saying words. Alina stopped listening. It was warm and dark under the blankets. Her breathing was fast. Heart pounding. Wanted to get away.

"Alina? You seem a little upset. Can you tell me what you're feeling right now? What's going on?"

"I don't want to go to school!" Alina said. "I don't want to be here."

"Okay," Melanie said. "I understand that. I know it can be scary to be in a new place. Lots of kids feel that way when they are brand new here. Are you feeling kind of scared?"

Alina's dream. Remembered. Scared feeling in her chest. Nodded under the covers.

"Was that a yes?" Melanie asked. "I think I saw your head move. Yes, I did," Melanie said playfully.

"Scared."

"Tell me what you're scared of."

Alina rocked. Tangled her fingers in her hair and pulled. Didn't answer. Didn't know.

"Let me see . . . are you worried about something happening in the classroom?"

"No," said Alina.

"Hmm. I wonder if . . ." Melanie said.

"Strangers," Alina blurted. "I don't like strangers."

"That makes sense. Strangers, people who are new to us, can be kind of scary. But you know what? I have an idea that might help."

Still breathing hard. Wanted to run. Wanted to believe Melanie. But couldn't. Still, Alina slowly lowered the blanket. She sat up, knees close to her chest, and squeezed her arms around her legs. Melanie standing by opposite wall. Smiled a little. Seemed nice.

"I see you have some pictures of Mom and Dad on your nightstand."

Alina looked at stack of pictures. Alina's last birthday. Mama and Papa next to Alina, laughing. Alina wearing a silver princess crown. Butterfly-shaped cake with *Happy birthday, Alina* written in purple letters. Alina reached for the picture. Ran fingers over Mama's brown hair.

"What if we picked your favorite pictures, and we could tape them to the inside of your notebook?" Melanie asked. "That way, when you're feeling a little scared of all the new people, you can look at them, and maybe you'll feel better. What do you think, Alina?"

Flicker of—something—inside Alina. Like the feeling when Mama put food on her plate and said, "Okay, honey, let's dig in."

Alina nodded. Quietly, she said, "Okay."

Melanie and Alina sat on floor, picking out pictures. Melanie helped Alina tape them to her fairy notebook. Walked with Alina to the bathroom and reminded her to wash face, brush teeth, like at home. Alina looked in mirror. Pale face, big eyes. Held notebook tight to chest as they walked down big empty hallway. Chest tight. Scared again. Opened notebook, saw Mama and Papa smiling. Stared at them as they walked. Alina and Melanie had breakfast together and then walked to school.

"Okay," Melanie said, stopping at a closed door. "Here we are."

Melanie opened door. Classroom. Seven kids, four grown-ups. Three grown-ups standing near other kids. One of them rubbing a boy's back. The fourth grown-up stood at the front of the room, by the white board.

"Alina, this is your teacher, Ms. Jane," Melanie said. "This is Anthony, her instructional aide. Hi, guys, I want to introduce you to Alina. She's new to Genesee Lake School and your classroom."

Ms. Jane smiled. "Welcome, Alina! We have a desk for you right over here, but if you're not comfortable with that, just let me know. We have some standing desks, too, and some kids also sit on big therapy balls. Okay, boys and girls, let's say hi to Alina!"

Four of the kids said "Hello!" and "Nice to meet you, Alina!" Three of the kids said nothing.

Alina looked around. One boy on the floor, in front of all the desks. No one yelled at him or made fun of him. One girl sat on a red cushion on her chair. Another boy, bouncing on a big blue ball. Classroom wasn't bright; it was dim, almost like nap-time. There was a lot to look at all over and on the walls. Alina sat down at her desk. Stared at her hands.

Melanie crouched down. "Alina, you're going to have a great day. Remember, if you start to feel upset, you can look at your pictures, and then I'll see you today after school, okay?"

"Okay," Alina whispered.

"We're all here to help you. You're going to have a good day." Melanie smiled and waved to Ms. Jane. Ms. Jane smiled and waved back. Melanie left room, closing door gently.

"Okay!" Ms. Jane said. "Let's get started, boys and girls! Alina, we always like to start the day with some breathing exercises. This helps to relax us if we're ever feeling worried or stressed."

Alina glanced up. Other kids, fidgeting in their seats, shrugging their shoulders and moving their heads.

"Who wants to lead the group today?" Ms. Jane asked.

Girl on other side of room jumping out of her seat. Hand darting up, yelling loudly, "Me! Me! Me!"

"Okay, Gaby." Ms. Jane's voice, low and slow. "Let's try to calm down just a little. Focus and slow your breathing. Come on up to the front of the room."

Girl ran to front of classroom. Laughing and jumping up on her toes. Ms. Jane gave her a weird wire thing to hold. "Go ahead, Gaby."

"Deep breath," girl said. "Breathe in. *Expand.*"

Girl tried to breathe but kept laughing. Fingers pulling wire thing apart when she breathed in, then closing it together when she breathed out.

"Slow it down, Gaby," Ms. Jane said. "Breathe in, slowly. A big, controlled breath."

A few more minutes. Classroom quiet. Girl stopped laughing. Everyone breathing. Alina breathing like she always breathed.

"Great job, everyone, and great job, Gaby. How about we tell Gaby thank you," Ms. Jane said. The rest of the class clapped their hands for a few seconds.

Ms. Jane said, "Thanks, Gaby. You can go back to you seat now. Great job."

Girl smiled, clapped, and jumped up and down, hurrying back to desk.

"Now, how about some imagery? Alina, you probably haven't done this before, but all you have to do is put your head on your desk and close your eyes."

Alina didn't like closing her eyes. Didn't like not seeing.

"Okay, boys and girls," Ms. Jane said. "We're about to go on a flight over North America. On the count of three, imagine that your chairs are lifting off from the floor. One . . . two . . . three! I'm pushing a button, and the roof of this classroom is sliding right off to let us pass. Now we're rising . . . we're flying above school now, reaching the tops of those tall trees outside. When we look down, we can see cars and grass and people walking."

Alina fidgeted. Other kids looked like they were sleeping. She didn't understand.

"Okay, we're flying higher and higher now. We're high above the United States now. Can you feel the clouds around us? Now, remember our lesson yesterday—clouds are made of drops of water and ice . . ."

Alina just sat still.

Lunchtime was later.

Lunchtime, teachers walked them to the cafeteria. Big

room, bright with sun through a wall of windows. Room filled with tables, tables filled with kids. More kids in a long line for food. Alina's belly growled. Smells filled her nose. Bread, spaghetti sauce, meat. She didn't think. Bolted toward front of the line, pushing another girl aside.

"Hey!" Girl stumbled, made a mean face at Alina. "You can't cut in line! I was here first."

Alina, be polite, Mama said at home. *Wait for everyone else to get their food before you start eating.*

But grabbed a tray and pushed forward again. Then—

"Ow!" Alina wailed. Spun around. Girl grabbing her hair, yanking hard. "Stop!"

Sounds disappeared. Alina's heart pounded so fast it made her dizzy. Didn't think. Reached out and scratched her nails down other girl's cheek. Red lines standing out on her white skin.

"Girls, stop! Michelle and Alina, stop right now!"

Samantha appeared, stepped between them with her hands in the air. Someone else talked quick to Michelle and walked away with her. Alina panting, hands in fists. Looked down. Dropped her tray. Wanted to pick up, didn't want to lower her head.

"Alina, you seem pretty upset," Samantha said. "Let's move out of line, and we can find some place to calm down. Sound good?"

Alina's gaze wild around the room: Samantha, kids in line—staring—food behind glass, cafeteria workers, kids eating—staring. Samantha moved away a little. Alina didn't know what to do. Took one step toward Samantha. Still breathing fast, heart still pounding.

"You're doing great," Samantha said. "How about some water? Getting a drink of water is soothing and helps a lot of people when they are upset. Would that help you feel better?"

A trick? Alina stared at Samantha. Samantha's arms by her sides, smiling, fingers open. Nodded. "Water," Alina said.

"Okay, just wait right here. You going to be okay until I'm back?" asked Samantha.

"Yes," said Alina.

"Great. I'll be right back with water."

Alina stood stiffly. Muscles tense. Ready. Samantha came back, handed Alina a cup of water with a straw.

"Try sipping it slowly," Samantha said. "Count to three in your head as you sip."

Alina wanted to gulp. Forced herself to sip slowly. *One . . . two . . . three.*

"Are you feeling better?"

Both hands gripping cup, straw in her mouth. Alina seeing more clearly. Sounds coming back. She nodded.

"Good." Samantha smiled. "Is it kind of hard to calm down when you're upset?"

Would she get in trouble?

"It's okay if it is. A lot of people struggle with that. But there are things we can do to help."

Alina gave one short nod. Gulped water. Tried to sip more slowly.

"Why don't we get back in line while we think this through?" Samantha took a step. Gestured for Alina to walk with her. Alina followed. "Sometimes, if we can understand what makes us upset, we can learn to problem solve or cope with those things when they happen. When you were in line for lunch, do you have any idea what happened to make you upset?"

One word came to Alina's mind. Made her feel bad. "Hungry," she said. "I was hungry."

Samantha nodded. "You were hungry. Of course. Great job telling me what you were thinking. Tell me, though, did anything else bother you or worry you about being in line?"

"I wanted food."

"Well, remember how we talked about how we show respectful behavior and language towards others? It's not showing good respect when we cut in line or push other kids. I'm just trying to help with this, Alina. Anything else about being in line that was a problem? You're not in trouble."

They were at back of line again. Alina's chest swelled with frustration. "So far away!" she burst out. "I want it now! Before it's gone."

"Oh, I see!" Samantha said. Line moved forward. "So what I'm hearing you say is that you were worried the food might be gone if you had to wait in line. Is that right?"

Alina nodded.

"Well, I can make you feel better about that. You don't have to worry about that, Alina," Samantha said. "The kitchen staff make enough food for everyone here. We never run out."

Samantha, lying. Food could always run out, Alina knew.

"What do you think might work better to handle things when you're feeling upset?" Samantha asked.

"Don't know," said Alina, head down.

"Some of our kids here ask to take a break sometimes, so they can be alone for a minute and calm down. Would that maybe work for you?"

Alina thought about it. Didn't like to be with people but didn't like to be alone. Not calming. Shook her head.

"Okay. How about taking a break and then also drinking a glass of water? Would that be helpful, Alina?"

Alina looked at her glass. A little water left. She drank it and nodded. Water made her feel better.

Samantha smiled. "That's great to know. Let's give it a try next time. Thanks for telling me about this—I know you much better now." Front of line, trays stacked, food steaming. "Well, here we are—what would you like for lunch?"

CHAPTER 23
A NEW NORMAL

At first, it was as though Alina were still at home. There was a tense hush in the house that, ironically, amplified every sound: the running of water, footsteps on the stairs, the television volume, the microwave beeps. Julie flinched with each break of the silence. It didn't occur to her until she and Mark were absently watching a war movie one night that she was behaving like a traumatized soldier herself, taken back to battle with every surprising *pop!* Once she made that connection, she realized with horror that was how they were all behaving. Mark still worked late, opening the front door as quietly as possible when he arrived home. (Julie hadn't realized until now how hard he worked at avoiding detection in order to not upset the balance in the house.) Luke ate his meals quickly so he could disappear upstairs or leave the house entirely. He never ventured into common areas for long. And Margaret whispered more than she spoke out loud, her eyes flitting paranoiacally around her. They had all positioned themselves around Alina's moods, desperately trying to avoid the landmines and explosions of her rage. But there could be no connection or growth in continued avoidance. Julie wasn't positive how to close that gap, but she had an idea..

"Mark," she said one night after dinner, "we need to talk."

"Uh oh," Mark said dryly. "I know what that means. What am I doing wrong this time?"

They were walking around their neighborhood, bundled in jogging pants and sweatshirts. Dry leaves skittered across the pavement as the sun lowered in the sky. Julie sensed the first snow was around the corner.

"Now that Alina is getting the help she needs at Genesee Lake School," said Julie, "I think you and I also need some help and changes."

"Don't you think we've made enough changes?" Mark tried to keep his voice light, but they both felt the tension beneath his words.

"We're not the family we used to be or the family we thought we'd become," Julie said. "We're all so . . . far apart. If we let it keep going like this, Luke will go away to college and never look back, and God knows what scars Margaret will have and hold against us later."

They turned left at the corner, lifting their hands in greeting at another couple who passed them, walking a panting golden retriever. In the fading light, Mark's face looked lined and tired.

"What are you suggesting?" he asked.

"We need counseling or family therapy or a support group—something that will help us focus on our marriage and where the rest of us fit within the family"

They walked quietly for another block, until their house came into view. Then Mark sighed. "I can't say I'm excited to talk to *more* therapists," he said, "but I agree we're only moving further apart. Let's do it."

The first call Julie made was to Dr. Brook. She had been so helpful with Alina that Julie was sure she'd be able to provide some suggestions. Sure enough, Dr. Brook gave her the names of three couples therapists and the contact information for one support group specifically for families of children with reactive attachment disorder. The group meeting was held once monthly, and the drive was almost an hour away, but Julie felt it was worth the attempt. Quickly, with more energy and determination than she realized she possessed, she compared the online backgrounds of three therapists and made a decision based on what her gut told her was the best fit for her and Mark.

The support group was small—other than Julie and Mark, there were three mothers and one father present. They sat on folding chairs with worn blue cushions in an offshoot of a church meeting hall. Neither Julie nor Mark had ever been to such a meeting before, and Julie found herself drawing references to Alcoholics Anonymous scenes she'd seen in movies. Should she stand up? *Hi, my name is Julie, and I'm a failed parent?*

It turned out that Shauna, the support group leader, introduced Julie and Mark to the group. "They've just placed their daughter, Alina, in a residential school."

One of the mothers—a brunette with an ivory headband and vibrant blue eyes—smiled in welcome. "While you're here to learn, you probably also have a lot to teach us," she said. "Jordan over there and her husband have been trying to get the district to pay for residential treatment for over a year."

Jordan, who was dressed in a dark tracksuit, nodded. Her fingers were intertwined in her lap. "It's hard.

It feels like they're giving us the runaround on purpose. We have no other options, can't afford the cost, and they just don't want to pay."

"Before we have that conversation" Shauna interrupted gently, "I want to recognize that coming here is a big step for Julie and Mark. You two have probably felt very alone in your journey to this point—"

Julie nodded, her throat tightening with Shauna's understanding tone.

"—but here you'll see that there are many others who share similar experiences. I encourage you all to connect outside of these sessions. There is power in shared knowledge, shared experience—and not just for the kids."

Julie reached for Mark's hand and smiled, nodding. For the next hour, the group talked about a variety of subjects. Julie explained how painful it was to admit they couldn't give Alina the care she needed and how frustrating it had been to receive such negative messages from friends and family—*why do you bother, why don't you send her back, she's just a bad kid.* The others in the room nodded. They had heard the same comments.

"Bad kid," grunted the father in the room. "It's easy to throw a label on something you don't understand, that's what I say."

Mark gave a hard nod. Julie saw that he was swallowing repeatedly, the way he did when he tried to contain his emotions. This was the first time either of them had felt that anyone remotely understood or shared their experience—not just from a clinical perspective, but from a parent's point of view.

On the drive home, both she and Mark were wired and incredulous. "It seems so silly now," Julie said, "but until tonight, I felt we were the only parents in the world who knew what this felt like."

Mark gave her a sidelong glance and rested a hand on her thigh. She placed her palm over it and slipped her fingers between his. "I did, too," he said.

The therapy session was equally illuminating. Dr. Theresa Salazar was younger than Dr. Brook, with frizzy curls and narrow wire-framed glasses. She exuded energy but not hyperactivity, and offered them orange spice tea when they walked into her office.

"You have gone through some extraordinary challenges—as a couple, as individuals, and as a family," Dr. Salazar said. She sat on a small armchair across from the floral loveseat Julie and Mark occupied. "Whether you realize it or not, what you've been through has also been traumatic for *you*. And to cope with trauma, it often helps to turn off the 'processing' parts of your brain. We are in survival mode."

"Do you mean like Alina?" Julie blurted. "Fight, flight, or freeze?"

Dr. Salazar nodded, smiling gently. "You have both fought so hard. Now it's time to unpack what that's meant for your own relationships with each other, yourselves, and the rest of your family."

Slowly, between the monthly support group, weekly couples therapy, and emails back and forth with other parents of children with reactive attachment disorder, things started changing in the Ryan home. One Saturday, they made it a family project to bring in some of the boxed items from the garage that used to personalize their home. They chose three boxes.

"Best not to do them all before we see how Alina

reacts," Mark said, and asked Luke and Margaret to open them. Luke, who initially resisted the exercise, sliced through the masking tape with scissors and let Margaret peel back the cardboard in hushed suspense, as though it were Christmas. Julie and Mark hung back, watching.

"How about you guys choose where everything goes?" Mark said.

"Everything?" Margaret asked, looking at the picture frames, books, and knickknacks inside the boxes.

"Everything," Julie said, smiling.

"Why are we doing this?" Luke asked. "What's the point?"

"The point is that we are doing something as a family," Mark said. "I think we can all agree it's been too long since we've done that."

"Yeah, Dad," Luke muttered. "Like six years."

The barb, though not unexpected, stung Julie. "Let's just try this and see how it goes," she said, hating the pleading tone in her voice.

"Sure. Whatever, Mom."

Margaret looked between them, hefting a coffee table book in her small hands. "This . . ." she looked around. Her eyes lit when she spotted space on the TV console. "Here!"

Julie laughed. She never would have put the book there, but she said, "That looks like the perfect spot."

Together, they rebuilt their home. Books found places sideways on shelves and upright on tables. Mark lifted Margaret high enough to place knickknacks on top of the fridge, and Luke rebelliously placed figurines and photos everywhere but where he knew they'd gone before. When they were finished, the house looked subtly silly, decorated by directionless elves. Julie knew, realistically, that some of these things might have to go again once Alina came home, but for now, it felt too good to question.

"Do you miss her?" Julie asked Mark one night after dinner. They were taking their now-habitual walk around the neighborhood.

"We talk to her every day," Mark said, squinting against the sun.

"You know that's not the same."

He sighed. "I want to say I do. But I don't miss the way we were living. Jules, that was miserable. It almost wrecked us. We were almost done."

"I know."

"It's so hard to separate her from her behavior. So hard to know who Alina is apart from reactive attachment disorder."

They walked in silence for a few minutes, their footsteps a soft metronome against the pavement. Julie was quiet for a few moments. Finally, she said, "She's our daughter. Our little girl."

CHAPTER 24
PROGRESS

"Hey, Alina." Dr. Mike. Smiling. Dr. Mike was nice. Alina saw him sometimes in the halls, walking by. He waved and said hi. Sometimes she waved back. Also saw him in his office, like today. They with played puzzles and drew pictures. "How's your week been?"

Alina sat straight in her chair. "Fine," she said softly.

"Great. So tell me, how has school been going for you?"

"Good."

"Ms. Jane says you're doing super at talking, participating, and helping out in the classroom."

Alina didn't know how to respond. A lot of times, people said things, and she didn't know what to say back. It was confusing. What they wanted her to say back. So she didn't say anything.

"How about we draw some pictures today?"

Alina liked drawing. Liked holding a marker in her hand, sliding it across the paper. Liked making something that wasn't there before.

"Let's draw a house. Any kind of a house you'd like."

Alina nodded. Took the paper and box of markers Dr. Mike gave her and leaned over table. Thinking of her house with Mama and Papa. Drew a box, with a triangle on top. Front door with a big knob. A window. Curtains closed.

"Thanks, Alina." Dr. Mike looking at her drawing. Smiling at her. "You're good at this. How about drawing a tree?"

New page. Brown marker. The trunk. The branches. Green marker. Some leaves. Red marker. Other leaves. Trees had a lot of color. Dead branches, though.

"Great work, Alina. Now how about a person? Any kind of person you want."

Person. Alina bit her lip. Drew a circle, stick body and arms and legs. Long squiggly hair.

"Very good," said Dr. Mike. "How about one more? Can you draw me a picture of your family doing something?"

Family. Watching TV. Mama, Papa. Drew them first. Papa the biggest. Drew Mama in a red sweater. Used black for her hair. Papa with his glasses. Luke and Margaret. Luke she drew almost as big as Papa. Not smiling. Margaret, a little circle on the side. When she finished, she passed it to Dr. Mike.

Dr. Mike picked up the paper. Looked closely. Smiled at Alina. "Okay, tell me who is in this picture."

Alina pointed. "Mama. Papa. Luke. Margaret."

"Okay, I see. And where are you in the picture?"

"Me?" Alina felt her eyes get small. Shrugged. Took the paper and drew a small picture of a person on the far right side.

"Okay. And what are the people thinking and feeling in the picture?"

"Feeling?"

"Yes."

Again. Alina didn't know. It was a picture. Not real. She shrugged.

"Let's talk a little more about feelings," Dr. Mike said. "We all have them. They can be good ones, like feeling happy and excited, or not-so-good ones, like feeling sad and angry. Do you ever feel upset or angry, Alina?"

Alina slowly shook her head. Stared at her fingers. Long and white. Wrapped them around each other.

"It can be kind of hard to talk about these things, I know. The neat part is that while we get upset or angry, there are things we can do to help us cope, or solve the problem, and then feel better." Dr. Mike passed some papers across the table. Alina looked at them. They had pictures on them. Curious.

"All right, check this out," Dr. Mike said. "It's real simple and has three parts. The first part has to do with triggers, or things that happen to make us upset. The second part has to do with how your body feels and reacts when you're upset, and the last part is about what you and we can do to help you cope and feel better. Ready? We'll make this like a game. Okay?"

Alina nodded.

"We all get upset about things either a lot—" Dr. Mike made a thumbs up sign. "—a little—" He made his hand flat and shook it a bit. "—or not much at all," he said, making a thumbs down sign. "I know I get *real* upset—" He showed a thumbs up. "—when some driver has his high beams on and won't turn them off as he drives towards me."

"Like Papa does," Alina said quietly. She smiled.

"Your dad, too, huh?"

Alina nodded. The papers had writing and pictures. She stared a them.

"The first question is, then, what makes you pretty

upset? Let's take a look at the top row first. Do you see anything on here that makes you mad or sad or frustrated?"

Alina shrugged.

"Okay, let's go one by one. Would you say being touched makes you feel upset?" Alina saw a picture of hands holding each other's wrists. She pointed and nodded.

"Okay," Dr. Mike said. "Being touched makes you upset. That bothers a lot of our kids. Let's do some more. Maybe read the words and look at the pictures and show me what's a 'thumbs up.'"

Slowly at first, and then faster, Alina pointed to a lot of pictures: too many people, darkness, yelling, missing someone, being hungry, being tired, someone being mean.

"Awesome work, Alina," Dr. Mike said. "See, these things happen, and they are triggers for you becoming upset. What do you think of this so far? Kinda fun?" He smiled.

Alina looked down at the cartoon drawings. "I like the pictures."

"Yeah, pictures help a lot of our kids understand things a bit better," Dr. Mike said. "Let's look at the second page now. This is about how our body feels when we're upset. I know when I have the guy with the bright headlights on the road, I can feel my muscles tense up on the steering wheel and I breathe a little harder. What happens to your body when you're upset?"

Alina roved her eyes over the page. Recognized a few pictures: clenched teeth, hot face, loud voice, racing heart, breathing hard, running away. Seemed as if she were pointing at all of them. Felt bad. She was a bad girl. Why Mama and Papa sent her away.

"No more." Alina crossed her arms.

"It's all right, Alina. Sometimes it's tough to talk about these things, but it is important. How about we just circle the ones that are super thumbs up? Let's try that."

Alina wanted to finish this. She pointed at the pictures she recognized. Dr. Mike made circles around them.

"Great job, Alina. See? There's a pattern here. When you feel one of the things that makes you upset, your body reacts in certain ways. Now, let's look at this last page because I think it can be kind of fun."

Fun. Alina stared at him. Wanted to believe him.

"We all have things we can do to make us feel better when we're upset. Isn't that great? I know for me, when that driver has his bright lights on and I'm breathing faster, I slow down my breathing and take a few deep breaths. Kind of like what you guys do in Ms. Jane's class, isn't it?"

Alina nodded slowly.

"That helps me. Also, if I'm upset at home, I might go outside and throw the ball over and over again to my dog, Pearl. She loves to fetch tennis balls, Alina, and would do it for hours, I think."

Alina smiled. "I like dogs."

"You do? That's great. Dogs can make good friends. So, let's take a look at this—we get to figure out what might make you feel better when you're upset by one of those triggers. It's okay to get upset. We just have to remember that we have tools, or things to try, to make us feel better."

Alina still didn't want to. But she let Dr. Mike show her the last page.

"So, the last question—what makes you feel better? Do you see anything?"

At first, Alina didn't. "Nothing."

"How about a quiet place?"

Alina shrugged. Thought of her room. "In my bed. Under blankets."

"Great. What about drinking water? Samantha mentioned that worked well for you in the cafeteria."

Alina nodded, and they circled a few more: looking at pictures, counting to ten, listening to music.

"Great," Dr. Mike said. "You did such good work here. I'm going to tell Melanie and Samantha that we did this, and then Samantha or one of the other staff will do a neat art project with you so that maybe we can put all this in the wall of your room. That way, you can see it and use some of the tools when you're upset, and the staff will also be able to suggest some tools to try. We do this for all our kids. What we can also do is put this on a small card for you, and you can carry it in your pocket—kind of like a secret weapon for when you're feeling upset and not sure what to do to feel better. Your staff and teachers will also have a copy of this card so they know what your triggers might be and how to help. Sound like a good plan?"

Safety tools. Secret weapon. Alina let the words sit in her mind. She *didn't* like being upset. Would be nice to feel better. But—"I don't know."

"Let's try it out and see how it goes. We can always change things later." Dr. Mike stood up. Smiled. "How about a snack? I think it's about time for that, isn't it?"

Alina nodded. Followed him out the room.

...

School was not like school at home. After breathing exercises, Ms. Jane said it was time for handwriting. Alina liked handwriting. It was like drawing—pencil to paper. Making sure the lines were straight or evenly curved. Top of the capital letter touching the top line on the page; bottom of the letter resting on the bottom line. She hated when she did it wrong—when the letters were crooked or shaky. Erased. Started over.

"Great job, everyone," Ms. Jane said. "It's time to do our classroom jobs. Does everyone remember their job this week?"

Alina didn't look up. Still doing handwriting. Shuffling around her.

"Alina." Ms. Jane standing next to Alina. "That's good handwriting. Have you been practicing by yourself?"

Shyly, Alina nodded.

"I can tell. That's excellent. It's time for classroom jobs now. Remember your job this week?"

Everyone had different jobs. This week, Jeffrey, a bigger boy, set the back jacks—cushions—on the floor for calendar time. Calendar time was when they changed the calendar and talked about the day and news. Nora announced that she had an overnight visit with her parents and went to dinner in a restaurant. Gaby put the back jacks away. Sam passed out snacks during snack time.

"Sharpen pencils," said Alina.

"Great memory! How about you get that started, Alina?" Ms. Jane smiled.

Alina didn't want to stop handwriting. Crossed her arms but eventually got up to sharpen pencils.

After calendar time was reading time. Ms. Jane separated them into groups. Three with her, three with Anthony, one with one aide, one with the other aide. Did their lessons quietly, though sometimes Jeffrey got loud. When he was mad, he pushed chairs and desks. Clattering and shouting. Once, he kicked at Ms. Jane, and Anthony and another classroom staff walked with him to the comfort room to calm down. Alina didn't like when Jeffrey got loud. It was one of her triggers. She could feel her body go tight. She felt as if someone could break her if they tried. Her heart pounded.

Different groups went to the SMART room at different times for "movement activities," as Ms. Jane called them. Said "Large and fine motor activities and hand/eye coordination exercises help with learning—and they're fun!" They also went to the indoor playground. There were monkey bars and trampolines. A scooter and a ball pit. Big swings and big pads to jump on. Some kids dove deep into the ball pit, covering themselves up. Other kids rolled on the trampoline or jumped up high. Ms. Jane said the SMART room and the indoor playground helped get them ready for learning.

"Alina, why don't we do some helicopter spins?" Ms. Jane asked.

Alina stood by the back wall. She watched everybody but didn't like to do things in here. It was unfamiliar and scary. Didn't want to do things wrong. Thought Ms. Jane would get mad at her. She shook her head.

"I'll tell you what—why don't you try it just one time? Then you can do something else." Ms. Jane held her arms straight out, smiling at Alina. "One time."

Alina took two steps from the wall. Held her arms out like Ms. Jane.

"That's good. Let's spin to our right. Slowly . . . controlled . . ."

Alina imitated Ms. Jane. Focused on not spinning too big or too fast. Afterwards, she dropped her arms to her sides.

Ms. Jane smiled. "That was perfect, Alina. Thank you for doing that. What would you like to do now?"

Alina thought about it. There was a big swing in the sensory room. She liked being on her stomach while Ms. Jane pushed the swing. Ms. Jane asked her to say whether she wanted to be pushed harder or softer, faster or slower. Alina felt . . . in control. Of an adult. "Can we swing?"

"We can definitely swing."

Alina smiled, just a little, and followed Ms. Jane out the door.

CHAPTER 25
IMPROVEMENT

Julie and Mark had visited Alina every two weeks like clockwork, and while it took a while to see noticeable improvement, they'd been able to go from on-grounds visits to off-grounds visits. They'd even spent the night in a nearby hotel once with only one small meltdown. Alina was, for the first time since they'd adopted her, manageable.

Julie and Mark spoke with Melanie on the phone at least once a week and met with her in person at least once a month. Each time, they spoke about Alina's care and progress at Genesee Lake School. Melanie reviewed how it went each time she saw Alina during the week—once for individual therapy, once for a group session, and usually several times casually, either in the hallways, classroom, or group living area.

"How do you think those group therapy sessions have been going lately?" Julie asked one Saturday. She and Mark sat at the round table in Melanie's office. The room was comfortable and warm, and Julie unbuttoned her coat.

"We've been working on understanding emotional intensity—right now, anxiety or worry," Melanie said. "We find that, because of delayed social emotional skills, a lot of our kids don't understand the world of emotions well. The kids need help identifying what they're feeling, making sense of the experience, and expressing and coping with their emotions."

She pulled a small laminated card from Alina's folder and handed it to Julie. "Our staff also works on identifying rumbling, rage, and recovery for the kids."

Mark nodded. "I remember we talked about that when we dropped Alina off here." He looked at Julie. "That seems like so long ago."

Julie agreed. And when she thought back to the first time they'd walked these hallways, it was like revisiting the edges of another life.

"As you know, then," Melanie said, "the three R's—rumbling, rage, and recovery—are the three stages of a meltdown. The model was developed more for kids with Asperger's disorder, but it fits many kids—and adults like us—and is a good framework for our staff."

"So how's Alina doing with it all?" Julie asked.

"Alina has shown an ability to recognize some of her triggers, which are pretty similar to what you've told us and what we've seen. We've noticed that if we intervene during the rumbling phase—which might be a two, say, on her one to five anger scale—we can often prevent her from getting to a five. A five is rage—which she calls her 'dark dark time'—and means explosive behavior and aggression toward staff. She understands the one to five scale—the change of intensity represented by numbers—and seems to like thinking about it this way."

"I'm sorry," said Julie, holding up a hand. "Did you say she calls it 'dark dark time?' She never talked that way to us. Dark dark time? It sounds awful." Tears rose to

Julie's eyes as she thought about what her daughter must experience during those times of rage.

"She is developing a language for what's going on internally," Melanie said. "She is making meaning or sense out of her experience on *her* terms. Remember when we talked about the power lying within the individual? Dr. Mike likes to tell us that we want to make the inner experience symbolic—we adults can do it through language and younger children though play. Alina is finding the power to make her experience more symbolic by giving it a language, a meaning. Does that make any sense?" Melanie asked with a laugh.

"It does," said Julie, "and when you frame it that way, it seems highly significant, what she's doing."

"It is," Melanie said. "The important part is that she seems to be making progress in understanding and expressing some of her emotions. This is hard work for many of our kids."

"So when is the last time she reached something high, like a five, on her anger scale?" Mark asked.

"Well, on her scale, *dark dark time* is feeling out of control, which leads to aggressive behavior . . ." Melanie glanced at the folder. She ran a neat fingernail down the page. "It looks like it was three weeks ago."

"Three weeks?" Julie and Mark exclaimed, almost in unison.

Julie was surprised at her rush of emotion. One side of her was elated. Another was disbelieving, almost mistrusting. And a third side was . . . resentful? Yes. That was it. Why couldn't she have been the one to help her daughter? She'd tried harder than anybody, and everyone kept saying she was the expert on her kid—so why hadn't her efforts worked? She knew the feeling wasn't rational, but the old sense of failure stung anyway.

"Wait a minute," said Julie. "I'm having a hard time with this right now."

"What are you talking about, Julie?" Mark said, laughing. "She said Alina's last meltdown was three weeks ago—three weeks!"

"No, not that—that's wonderful." Julie took a deep breath, not sure why she was about to say her next words. "What I want to know is why everyone says I am the expert on my child, yet I tried so hard—*we* tried so hard, Mark, everyone did, the county, the public schools—and it didn't work and she had to leave our home and come here. This is a nice place, but it's not home, with her family." Julie felt breathless after her rush of emotion. Mark looked slightly embarrassed.

"You're not the only parents to struggle with these feelings," Melanie said. "This is where we circle back to collaborative problem solving, which believes that *we all want to do well in life*. Remember that the philosophy of collaborative problem solving is that kids do well if they *can*—not kids do well if they *want* to, which is what a lot of people in society believe. Think about it, then—this also means that parents want to do well in life, right?"

Julie and Mark nodded.

"So parents do well if they can. Yes, you are the experts on your child. You are extremely motivated, and no one has tried harder than you two—that exudes from you as we talk. The most important point for you to know is this: all the motivation in the world won't get the job done if we don't have the skills to accompany it. You are not failures. You have a daughter with significant attachment problems who has experienced complex and developmental trauma. As parents, you didn't have the skills to understand that trauma's impact on Alina's brain development or to make sense out of Alina's behavior in the context of underdeveloped skill development. Without that understanding, it would have been impossible to intervene effectively.

"Further," Melanie continued, "you shouldn't even be expected to have these skills. At Genesee Lake School, we should, and do, have these skills. That's the biggest part of working with parents—the love is there; it's about helping them make sense of their kid. You wanted to adopt and love a child from Russia, to give a home and family to an abandoned child. You opened your hearts. Alina's needs are extremely complex, and you could not have been realistically expected to be successful on your own. Alina needs short-term residential therapeutic services to help develop those social, emotional, and cognitive—including self-regulation—skills. Skills that you will be able to support and enforce when she returns home. She needs this for a while, not forever. You aren't failures. You are champions."

Melanie's face wore a slight flush after her speech. Julie was moved by how strongly Melanie believed in them and validated their efforts. She felt her chest ease slightly in relief, and when Melanie smiled and suggested they take a break for coffee, Julie nodded gratefully.

When they returned to the room, they picked up where they had left off with Alina's one to five anger scale and her last incidence of a five.

"The dark dark time was during her morning routine," Melanie said. "That tends to be the most difficult time of day for Alina."

"We remember it well," Mark said dryly, looking at Julie.

"Since we recognize it takes her extra time to get going in the morning, she's among the first that the staff wake up. These are basic behavioral supports, focusing on changing the antecedent condition of the behavior. Pretty basic but powerful for behavior problems, and we find that once you pay close attention to the child and read her cues, you can figure out what to tweak on the front end to change what happens on the back end. With the morning routine, we've found that waking her up first often prevents her from being late for class. That wasn't so successful, though, several weeks ago."

"How long did it last?" Julie asked.

"Two and a half hours."

Julie winced, imagining the chaos. "I'm sorry."

Melanie smiled. "There's no need to apologize. We have to remember that kids with significant emotion regulation problems—like your daughter—don't *like* being upset and showing explosive or implosive behavior. And they're certainly not doing it on purpose."

"I know that," Julie said. "Even when she was at her worst, it was always clear how bad she felt afterwards."

"It must be miserable," Melanie agreed. "The key is to remember that if you can intervene during the rumbling stage with support, sensory strategies, and access to coping and calming strategies, you'll see a significant reduction in explosive behavior because she will often not even reach the rage state."

"In this case, though," Mark said, "she obviously made it to the rage state anyway. Were there any negative consequences afterwards?"

"Negative consequences have side effects," Melanie

answered. "With collaborative problem solving, those consequences are one way to pursue expectations, but they don't teach thinking skills or solve the problem durably. Most importantly for kids with complex trauma, they don't heal and strengthen relationships to rework versions of self, others, and the world. Negative consequences actually impair and weaken the relationship because they confirm that the power is with the adult, not the child. The relationship is not therapeutic; and social, emotional, and relational growth and repair are hindered. So, from a trauma-informed care perspective, we avoid punishment-based methods. We try to teach skills instead. Don't get me wrong, though," she added, "teaching skills is hard work, and it takes time. But like we tell our staff, if you want a strong bicep, what do you have to do?"

"Lift weights," Mark replied.

"Right. Same thing with kids and skills. If you want a child to get better at problem solving, then solve real life problems to work on those skills. It seems to resonate with parents when we remind them that someday their child is going to be thirty years old, so what matters now is not their diagnosis. Diagnosis has its place—mostly for professionals and, honestly, for billing insurance companies—but it doesn't tell us what skills the kid lacks and what to do in here and now to teach those skills."

Mark exhaled. "She'll be thirty one day," he repeated, shaking his head. "Oh, boy."

"So with the morning routine," Julie ventured, "has trying to solve the problem collaboratively worked?"

"Not totally," Melanie said, smiling. "Real life problems are rarely solved overnight, and Alina brings some real problem-solving deficits to the table. But we're making progress."

"I'm so glad we found your school." Julie shook her head. "As combustible as we felt then, I can see now how truly on the verge of breakdown we were. I don't know how much longer we would have lasted, as a family."

Mark took her hand and squeezed. "Thank you," he said to Melanie.

Melanie smiled. "Let's go see Alina."

CHAPTER 26
BETTER

"Mama! Papa!"

Alina rushed to them when she saw them at her door. Mama wrapped her arms around Alina and pulled her close. Alina tucked her head into Mama's shoulder. Held another arm out to hug Papa's waist. Every time they came, she was . . . not sure. She thought of the pictures Melanie always showed her and the ones that were up in the group living area. Faces showing different emotions. Surprised. She was surprised, and she was happy.

They took Alina outside to the playground. The sun was shining. Warm on Alina's face and bright in her eyes. She squinted at Mama as Papa pushed her on the swing.

"What have you been learning at school?" Mama asked. Touched Alina's knees as the swing moved forward.

"Friend behavior and not-friend behavior," Alina said. Swung backwards. Papa's hands firm on her back.

"Friend behavior! What's that?"

"I picked up Gaby's pencil." The cool breeze made tears prick Alina's eyes. "Ms. Jane said that was good friend behavior. Jeffrey hit Sam because Sam got in his way. That was not-friend behavior."

"That's really good," Mama said. Smiling big. "And have you made any friends?"

Alina moved her shoulders up and down. Holding swing. "I don't know. I talk to Gaby sometimes. She's silly."

They played outside a little longer, and then they ate in the cafeteria. Mama and Papa left when it got dark outside. They hugged her and kissed her forehead.

"We are so proud of you," Papa said. Moved her hair away from her face. "Do you know that?"

Proud. Alina didn't know what proud meant. "I love you," she said instead.

"We love you, too, honey."

Alina was sad when Mama and Papa were gone. They always said, "We'll see you in two weeks and talk to you tomorrow." But she could never be sure.

On Monday, when Samantha came to wake her up, she pulled the blankets over head. Squeezed her eyes shut. Pretended she didn't hear Samantha. *Go away*, she thought. *Go away, go away, go away.*

"Alina, you know the routine," Samantha said. "It's time for your shower and then breakfast so you aren't late for school. You know how happy Ms. Jane is when you're on time."

"I don't care," Alina said. But that wasn't true. She liked making Ms. Jane happy. She just didn't like getting out of bed in the morning. The air and floor were cold. They reminded her of being little. Cold made her also feel hungry. She grunted. Rolled into a ball. When she didn't hear Samantha, she lowered the covers. Peeked out. Samantha, standing quietly.

Alina was late again for school that day. She had yelled at Samantha. Eyes felt like they were burning. She felt bad.

Ms. Jane didn't get mad, though. On the board, she was writing out words.

"We're going to be working on character traits for the next several weeks," she said. "Character traits are what make up your personality. There are positive and negative character traits. A positive character trait might be *nice*. So a negative one would be . . ."

"Mean!" Gaby exclaimed. Clapped her hands. She liked talking in class.

"Good." Ms. Jane wrote *Nice* and *Mean* on two sides of the board. "What are some other positive character traits? Jeffrey?"

Jeffrey, bouncing on a therapy ball. "Patient?"

"Good. That's excellent. Nora?"

Nora always sat on the red cushion. Played with a fidget toy. "Respectful?"

"Yes. That's a great one. How about you, Alina?"

Alina froze. She didn't like talking in class. Didn't like being called on. She shrugged. Looked away.

"Alina, you can do it. It's one word," Ms. Jane said.

Alina thought of Mama. "Kind," she whispered.

"Kind. Yes." Ms. Jane smiled. "Very good."

• • •

"Hey there, Alina." Samantha, walking up to her in group room. Smiling. "How are you doing today?"

Alina shrugged. Hands holding book with hard shiny cover. Looking at Samantha. "Okay," she said quietly.

"Yeah, what are you reading?"

Alina closed the book cover. Held it out to Samantha.

"*Oh, The Places You'll Go*," Samantha said. "That's a good one. Do you like Dr. Seuss?"

Alina shrugged again. Mama read some Dr. Seuss. Alina in Mama's lap. Alina remembered *Hop on Pop*. She liked that. "Yeah," Alina said.

"Well, good. I'll make sure we've got enough Dr. Seuss for you then." Samantha smiled. Sat on the floor in front of Alina's chair. Legs folded. "Hey, I wanted to talk to you about something for a minute. Would that be okay?"

Alina stared down at her. Not knowing what was coming. Alina didn't like not knowing. It scared her.

"You're not in trouble," Samantha said. "I just want to talk to you about the morning routine."

Alina picked up her book again. "I don't want to."

"Alina, you know one of the things we do here when problems come up is try to think them through, so we can solve the problem together. It's not going so well when it's time to start the morning routine—what's up?"

Alina shook her head. Flipped pages.

"I know, maybe not easy to talk about. You're not in trouble, though," Samantha said, "and no one's mad. I just want to know what's going on."

"I don't know," Alina said. "I don't want to talk."

"Let's think about it a bit. Tell me what happened this morning."

Alina read words in the book: *Today . . . is . . . your . . . day.*

"Alina?"

Alina looked at Samantha. Still sitting on floor, arms by her sides. Smiling. A moment passed. "It's cold," Alina said.

"It's cold? Does that have something to do with why it's hard to get up in the morning? Can you tell me more so I can understand better?"

Alina nodded. "I don't like it. It's nice and warm in my bed, and it's cold when I get up. I don't like it."

"Well, let me make sure I got this right. You feel comfortable and warm in bed in the morning, and when staff come to wake you up to get ready, you know it will be colder when you get up—and then it's more hard to get up. Do I have it right?"

Alina nodded.

"Great, thanks. The thing is, Alina, when this happens, you're often late to Ms. Jane's classroom, which means you're not doing your work and learning, and because one of the staff has to stay with you, they also aren't able to get to their classroom on time, which make is hard to provide supervision. Let's think this through. I wonder if there's a way that you can feel more comfortable and warm in the morning at wake-up so you're not late for school and the staff are able to supervise in the classroom on time. Do you have any ideas?"

Alina shrugged.

"It can be hard to figure out solutions, but let's try. We're looking for some way that you can feel more comfortable and warm in the morning at wake-up, not be late for school, and staff can also be to school on time. Got an idea?"

Alina thought of home. There was a fireplace. "Make a fire in my room."

Samantha nodded. "Every idea is a good idea, but we have to take a look at it. It needs to work for you, work for us, and be doable," she said. "Making a fire in your room might seem like it could work for you, but it doesn't work for us because it would be unsafe for you and the rest of the kids, and safety is important, right?"

Alina nodded.

"What might be another idea?" asked Melanie. "Remember, every idea is a good idea, and we'll just take a look at it. Go for it!"

Alina chewed the inside of her cheek. "I can get dressed under the blankets?"

Samantha clapped her hands. "There's an idea. How would that work?"

"My clothes are picked out the night before, and then I get dressed under the covers?" asked Alina.

"Well it sounds like it works for you, and I know it works for us, and I'm the supervisor up here, so I definitely know it's doable. So how about we give it a try? Maybe start tomorrow morning and see how it goes?"

"Yes," said Alina and smiled.

"Great, I'll let the staff know. Karen is working tonight, so she'll help you pick out those clothes and get things ready. Great job, Alina!"

"Thanks," Alina said, smiling again.

That night, Alina stood in her closet with Karen and chose what to wear the next day. Pulled out jeans, a long-sleeve purple shirt, and a white zip-up sweater. Carefully, so they wouldn't wrinkle, she lay them at the foot of the bed. She pulled out one corner of the sheets so she could reach for them in the morning. And when Samantha woke her up, and Alina was cold, she slipped one hand out and slid the clothes toward her. She was still tired. She still didn't like mornings. But it was better.

CHAPTER 27
IF I WERE PRESIDENT

When Alina had been at Genesee Lake School for one year, Julie got a call from Melanie that, on some level, she'd never expected to receive.

"Now that Alina's made good progress in our center building, we'd love to meet with you and Mr. Ryan to discuss Alina moving to a less restrictive setting in one of our group homes. We think she's ready."

Julie was in the passenger seat as Luke, now sixteen, drove Julie's SUV to the University of Wisconsin-Madison. The sky was white and faded blue through the windshield, in that transition from winter's heaviness, and Julie could hardly believe it was time for Luke to apply to colleges. Now it also seemed that her daughter growing up.

"A less restrictive environment at a Genesee Lake School group home?"

"Exactly. The one we have in mind is nearby in the community, so it's still close, and Alina would have much more independence. She'll have a roommate, daily chores, learn how to do her own laundry, and help prepare meals. Essentially, she'll learn many of the basic living skills that will help her transition successfully back to your home one day."

Julie was silent, and Luke gestured questioningly toward an upcoming exit. Julie nodded, and he carefully switched on the blinker and eased into the far right lane.

"Are you sure she's ready? Will she be safe?" Julie asked. Alina had made progress; that was undeniable. But her overnight visit the previous month had been fraught with tension after Julie had said no to going to the zoo. While it wasn't nearly as extreme as it used to be, Alina had thrown a fit for an hour before shutting down. What if she wasn't as ready for this as Melanie thought? What if she raged and hurt herself or someone else, or decided to just . . . leave?

"We have at least two staff with the kids all the time," Melanie said. "That's the same coverage as here at the center building. More importantly, if we didn't feel that Alina was already showing good self-control and safe behavior, we wouldn't even think about this kind of move right now. Also, the transition process to a group home occurs over time and at her pace—so we'll start with short visits, spending time with the other kids, maybe go see a movie with them, give her some pictures of the group home to ease into group home living, things like that."

The university where Julie and Mark had met two decades earlier approached, and Luke was trying hard to contain a full-faced grin. He gestured to Julie again, asking where he should park.

"Let's talk more about this on Friday," Julie said. "Mark and I will be going up to see Alina. Does that work for you?"

"Of course." They set up a time to meet, and then Julie turned her full attention to her son.

...

More people than usual were at their meeting on Friday. Melanie had also invited Dr. Mike, the psychologist; Ms. Jane, Alina's teacher; and Samantha, the unit supervisor. Over the next hour, each of them told Julie and Mark about the progress they'd seen Alina make in her time at the center. Ms. Jane seemed especially fond of her.

"When she first started here, it was uncomfortable for her to talk—to me or anyone else," Ms. Jane said. "I asked her mostly yes or no questions in class, and she would nod or shake her head. As she started responding to me more, I began pushing her. 'You can answer me with a sentence.' That sort of thing. I've also found interests she enjoys, like drawing and practicing her handwriting, and built activities around those things. Harnessing her natural interests is a great way to build engagement."

"What Jane did was meet Alina where she was at," Dr. Mike said. "That's a big belief of ours. She didn't overwhelm her by forcing her to talk; she just took what she could and built on it incrementally. Over time, due to the positive classroom experiences and how Jane interacts with her—so, providing consistency, sensitivity, and certainty—Alina started to trust more."

Ms. Jane nodded. "Nothing has been quick or easy with her. It's just a matter of repetition over time. Oh!" She looked at Melanie and Dr. Mike, smiling. "I don't know if I'd told you guys. I gave the kids a writing prompt the other day. It was: 'If I were president, I would . . .'"

"And all the kids gave answers?" Dr. Mike asked.

Ms. Jane laughed. "Did they ever! Everything from 'I would have free video games for life' to 'I would fly to the moon.'"

"What did Alina write?" Julie asked.

"Yeah, what did our daughter have to say?" Mark chimed in.

"Alina said that if she were president, she would make sure everyone in the country had moms and dads."

For a moment, an almost magical hush fell over the room. Goosebumps rose on Julie's arms, and her throat tightened with tears.

"She—" Mark cleared his throat. "She wrote that?"

Ms. Jane smiled. "She did."

They talked more about the group home and how Genesee Lake School would help Alina with the transition over the coming months. Then Melanie walked them to Alina's room and gave the Ryans a warm smile.

"There's still a road ahead, you know," she said. "But Alina has come a long way from the start of her journey here."

...

On their overnight, Julie and Mark lay in bed next to Alina. They read to her from Dr. Seuss—which they were also reading to Margaret back home—until they saw Alina's eyelids start to flutter and then drop. Her fair lashes shivered against each other as she tried to keep her eyes open.

"Just go to sleep, honey," Julie whispered, kissing Alina's temple. Alina opened her eyes and stared at her for a moment with those mercurial eyes—the eyes that had seen so much, that had so often refused to close, that could contain so much rage and hurt—and then she shifted closer to Julie, snuggling against her side. Mark smiled at her over their daughter's relaxed body.

Alina slept. The Ryans slept.

CHAPTER 28
HAPPY

In the group room, Alina breathed deeply. Popcorn. Movie night later. Her stomach rumbled. She wanted it now. *Wait,* she thought. *It will not run out. Talk to Dr. Mike first.*

Dr. Mike waved, walking into the room. Alina lifted her hand, then lowered it back to her lap.

"Hey, Alina," Dr. Mike said. Sat on chair across from Alina. Smiled at her. She smiled back. "Nice to see you. So how's it going today?"

"Good," she said, with a smile and a little nod.

"I heard that you'll be moving to one of our group homes soon."

Alina listened. Was there a question? She nodded.

"So what do you think about that?"

She looked down. Chair had her name on the bottom: Alina. It was hers. She had cut the letters from construction paper. Her room also had her name and photo on the door. That was hers, too. They said she would get to decorate her side of the room at the group home the way she wanted. "Okay. I can take my pictures?"

"Of course you can take your pictures—they're yours. Hey, speaking of pictures, how about we do some drawings today? I know you love to draw. You can take them with you when you go to the group home, too."

Alina nodded. Went to the back of the room where there was paper and colored pencils. She sat down with the paper and pencils in front of her. Chose a purple pencil, her favorite color.

"What are we drawing?" she asked.

"Whatever we want." Dr. Mike squinted at the paper. Took a green pencil and made squiggly lines on the bottom of the page. He caught her looking and laughed. "I have a feeling you're much better at drawing than me. Look, a fish!" he said.

Alina cracked a smile. Dr. Mike was a bad drawer. His fish looked like a dog.

For a few minutes, they drew in silence. Popcorn smell got stronger. Voices and footsteps in the hallway. Alina didn't look up. She was drawing a fairy. She liked drawing fairies. Fairies could make magic happen. Made the wings big and curved and colored them light pink. Gave the fairy reddish yellow hair like Alina's, with blue eyes. Drew clouds around the fairy. She was flying.

"See this?" Dr. Mike showed Alina his drawing. "It's a boat on the water. That's what I like to do in the summer. Fish in a boat."

Alina looked at the drawing, then at Dr. Mike. She giggled. "That's not a boat."

"No? Really, it is."

She shrugged and smiled. "I'm not sure."

"Okay, how about we draw one more picture, Alina?" Dr. Mike asked, laughing.

"It's been a while since we've done this, but how about drawing a picture of your family?"

Alina looked at Dr. Mike and nodded. She started with Mama, then Papa. Made Papa too short. She erased and started over. Drew Luke, with messy hair and a base-ball cap. Then drew herself, pretty little next to Luke but taller than Margaret, to her right. Margaret with the same-color hair as Alina's. She drew lots of trees next to them with a square house behind them.

"That's a nice picture, Alina." Dr. Mike said quietly. "Where is everybody in this picture?"

"Home," she said.

"Your family is all together in the picture," said Dr. Mike.

She nodded, reaching for a green colored pencil to fill in the grass at their feet. Smiled. Springtime. Flowers were growing.

"What are they feeling?"

Alina glanced up at Dr. Mike. His brown eyes crinkled, sleeves rolled up a little. She looked back down at her drawing. Smiled. The five of them. Her family.

Softly, she said, "Happy."

HOW THESE BOOKS WERE CREATED

The ORP Library of disabilities books is the result of heartfelt collaboration between numerous people: the staff of ORP, including the CEO, executive director, psychologists, clinical coordinators, teachers, and more; the families of children with disabilities served by ORP, including some of the children themselves; and the Round Table Companies (RTC) storytelling team. To create these books, RTC conducted dozens of intensive, intimate interviews over a period of months and performed independent research in order to truthfully and accurately depict the lives of these families. We are grateful to all those who donated their time in support of this message, generously sharing their experience, wisdom, and—most importantly—their stories so that the books will ring true. While each story is fictional and not based on any one family or child, we could not have envisioned the world through their eyes without the access we were so lovingly given. It is our hope that in reading this uniquely personal book, you felt the spirit of everyone who contributed to its creation.

ACKNOWLEDGMENTS

The authors would like to thank the following team members at Genesee Lake School and ORP who generously lent their time and expertise to this book: special education teacher Jade Gorecki, licensed psychologist Anne Felden, and clinical coordinator Christy Lynch. Your passion, experience, and wisdom make this book an invaluable tool for other educators, families, and therapists. Thank you for your enthusiastic contributions to this project.

We would also like to extend our deepest gratitude to the families who invited us into their worlds (and, in some cases, their homes!). Chris Burrows, Lori and Karl Hetzel, and Marilyn Tauscher—the courage, ferocity, and love with which you shepherd your children through their lives is nothing short of heroic. Thank you for sharing your journeys with us, from the joy of adoption to the fear of the unknown to the hope for the future. You are the reason we are telling this story—and the only reason we could do so authentically.

And to readers of *An Unlikely Trust*—the parents committed to helping their children, the educators who teach those children skills needed for greater independence, the therapists who shine a light on what can be a frighteningly mysterious road, and the schools and counties that make difficult financial decisions to benefit these children: thank you. Your work is miraculous.

JEFFREY D. KRUKAR, PH.D.

BIOGRAPHY

Jeffrey D. Krukar, Ph.D. is a licensed psychologist and certified school psychologist with more than 20 years of experience working with children and families in a variety of settings, including community based group homes, vocational rehabilitation services, residential treatment, juvenile corrections, public schools, and private practice. He earned his Ph.D. in educational psychology, with a school psychology specialization and psychology minor, from the University of Wisconsin-Milwaukee. Dr. Krukar is a registrant of the National Register of Health Service Providers in Psychology, and is also a member of the American Psychological Association.

As the psychologist at Genesee Lake School in Oconomowoc, WI, Dr. Krukar believes it truly takes a village to raise a child—to strengthen developmental foundations in relating, communicating, and thinking—so they can successfully return to their families and communities. Dr. Krukar hopes the ORP Library of disabilities books will bring to light the stories of children and families to a world that is generally not aware of their challenges and successes, as well as offer a sense of hope to those currently on this journey. His deepest hope is that some of the concepts in these books resonate with parents and professionals working with kids with disabilities, and offer possibilities that will help kids achieve their maximum potential and life enjoyment.

KATIE GUTIERREZ

BIOGRAPHY

Katie Gutierrez believes that a well-told story can transcend what a reader "knows" to be real about the world—and thus change the world for that reader. In every form, story is transformative, and Katie is proud to spend her days immersed in it as executive editor for Round Table Companies, Inc.

Since 2007, Katie has edited approximately 50 books and co-written six—including *Meltdown*, one of the ORP Library of disabilities books. She has been humbled by the stories she has heard and hopes these books will help guide families on their often-lonely journeys, connecting them with resources and support. She also hopes they will give the general population a glimpse into the Herculean jobs taken on so fiercely by parents, doctors, therapists, educators, and others who live with, work with, and love children such as Alina.

Katie holds a BA in English and philosophy from Southwestern University and an MFA in fiction from Texas State University. She has contributed to or been profiled in publications including *Forbes*, *Entrepreneur* magazine, *People* magazine, *Hispanic Executive Quarterly*, and *Narrative* magazine. She can't believe she's lucky enough to do what she loves every day.

JAMES G. BALESTRIERI

BIOGRAPHY

James G. Balestrieri is currently the CEO of Oconomowoc Residential Programs, Inc. (ORP). He has worked in the human services field for 40 years, holding positions that run the gamut to include assistant maintenance, assistant cook, direct care worker, teacher's aide, summer camp counselor, bookkeeper, business administrator, marketing director, CFO, and CEO. Jim graduated from Marquette University with a B.S. in Business Administration (1977) and a Master's in Business Administration with an emphasis in Marketing (1988). He is also a Certified Public Accountant (Wisconsin—1982). Jim has a passion for creatively addressing the needs of those with impairments by managing the inherent stress among funding, programming, and profitability. He believes that those with a disability enjoy rights and protections that were created by the hard-fought efforts of those who came before them; that the Civil Rights movement is not just for minority groups; and that people with disabilities have a right to find their place in the world and to achieve their maximum potential as individuals. For more information, see *www.orp.com*.

ABOUT ORP

Oconomowoc Residential Programs, Inc. is an employee-owned family of companies whose mission is to make a difference in the lives of people with disabilities. Our dedicated staff of 2,000 employee owners provides quality services and professional care to more than 1,700 children, adolescents, and adults with special needs. ORP provides a continuum of care, including residential therapeutic education, community-based residential services, support services, respite care, treatment programs, and day services. The individuals in our care include people with developmental disabilities, physical disabilities, and intellectual disabilities. **Our guiding principle is passion:** a passion for the people we serve and for the work we do. For a comprehensive look at our programs and people, please visit *www.orp.com*.

ORP offers two residential therapeutic education programs and one alternative day school among its array of services. These programs offer developmentally appropriate education and treatment for children, adolescents and young adults in settings specially attuned to their needs. We provide special programs for students with specific academic and social issues relative to a wide range of disabilities, including autistic disorder, Asperger's disorder, mental retardation, anxiety disorders, depression, bipolar disorder, reactive attachment disorder, attention deficit disorder, Prader-Willi syndrome, and other disabilities.

Genesee Lake School is a nationally recognized provider of comprehensive residential treatment, educational, and vocational services for children, adolescents, and young adults with emotional, mental health, neurological, or developmental disabilities. GLS has specific expertise in Autism Spectrum Disorders, anxiety and mood disorders, and behavioral disorders. We provide an individualized, person-centered, integrated team approach, which emphasizes positive behavioral support, therapeutic relationships, and developmentally appropriate practices. Our goal is to assist each individual to acquire skills to live, learn, and succeed in a community-based, less restrictive environment. GLS is particularly known for its high quality educational services for residential and day school students.

Genesee Lake School / Admissions Director
36100 Genesee Lake Road
Oconomowoc, WI 53066
262-569-5510
http://www.geneseelakeschool.com

T.C. Harris School is located in an attractive setting in Lafayette, Indiana. T.C. Harris teaches skills to last a lifetime, through a full therapeutic program as well as day school and other services.

T.C. Harris School / Admissions Director
3700 Rome Drive
Lafayette, IN 47905
765-448-4220
http://tcharrisschool.com

The Richardson School is a day school in West Allis, Wisconsin that provides an effective, positive alternative education environment serving children from Milwaukee and the surrounding communities.

The Richardson School / Director
6753 West Roger Street
West Allis, WI 53219
414-540-8500
http://www.richardsonschool.com

RESOURCES

Allen, Jeffrey S., and Roger J. Klein. *Ready . . . Set . . . R.E.L.A.X.: A Research Based Program of Relaxation, Learning, and Self-Esteem for Children.* Watertown, WI: Inner Coaching, 1996.

American Association of Children's Residential Centers. *Redefining Residential: Trauma-Informed Care in Residential Treatment.* Position Paper. Milwaukee, WI: American Association of Children's Residential Centers, 2010.

American Psychiatric Association. *Diagnostic and Statistical Manual of Mental Disorders, Fourth Edition, Text Revision.* Washington, DC: American Psychiatric Association, 2000.

Blaustein, Margaret E., and Kristine M. Kinniburgh. *Treating Traumatic Stress in Children and Adolescents: How to Foster Resilience through Attachment, Self-Regulation, and Competency.* New York: The Guilford Press, 2010.

Buron, Kari D., and Mitzi Curtis. *The Incredible 5-point Scale: Assisting Students with Autism Spectrum Disorders in Understanding Social interactions and Controlling Their Emotional Responses.* Shawnee Mission, KS: Autism Asperger Publishing Co., 2003.

Greene, Ross W. *The Explosive Child.* New York: Harper Collins Publishers, 2005.

Greene, Ross W., and J. Stuart Ablon. *Treating Explosive Kids: The Collaborative Problem-Solving Approach.* New York: The Guilford Press, 2006.

Greenspan, Stanley, and Serena Wiedera. *The Child with Special Needs: Encouraging Intellectual and Emotional Growth.* Cambridge, MA: Da Capo Press, 1998.

IDEA – Building the Legacy: IDEA 2004, *http://idea.ed.gov.*

Interdisciplinary Council on Developmental and Learning Disorders, *http://www.icdl.com.*

Massachusetts Department of Mental Health "Restraint/Seclusion Reduction Initiative: Safety Tool," *http://www.mass.gov/dmh/rsri.*

Siegel, Daniel J., and Tina Payne Bryson. *The Whole Brain Child: 12 Revolutionary Strategies to Nurture Your Child's Developing Mind.* New York: Delacorte Press, 2011.

Smith Myles, Brenda, and Jack Southwick. *Asperger Syndrome and Difficult Moments: Practical Solutions for Tantrums, Rage, and Meltdowns.* Shawnee Mission, KS: Autism Asperger Publishing Co., 2005.

Think:Kids, Rethinking Challenging Kids, *http://www.thinkkids.org.*

van der Kolk, Bessel A. "Developmental Trauma Disorder: Toward a Rational Diagnosis for Children with Complex Trauma Histories." *Psychiatric Annals,* 35 (2005): 401–408.

REACTIVE ATTACHMENT DISORDER

An Unlikely Trust: Alina's Story of Adoption, Complex Trauma, Healing, and Hope, and its companion children's book, *Alina's Story,* share the journey of Alina, a young girl adopted from Russia. After living in an orphanage during her early life, Alina is unequipped to cope with the complexities of the outside world. She has a deep mistrust of others and finds it difficult to talk about her feelings. When she is frightened, overwhelmed, or confused, she lashes out in rages that scare her family. Alina's parents know she needs help and work endlessly to find it for her, eventually discovering a special school that will teach Alina new skills. Slowly, Alina gets better at expressing her feelings and solving problems. For the first time in her life, she realizes she is truly safe and loved . . . and capable of loving in return.

AN UNLIKELY TRUST

ALINA'S STORY OF ADOPTION,
COMPLEX TRAUMA, HEALING,
AND HOPE

ALINA'S STORY

LEARNING HOW TO TRUST,
HEAL, AND HOPE

ASPERGER'S DISORDER

Meltdown and its companion comic book, *Melting Down*, are both based on the fictional story of Benjamin, a boy diagnosed with Asperger's disorder and additional challenging behavior. From the time Benjamin is a toddler, he and his parents know he is different: he doesn't play with his sister, refuses to make eye contact, and doesn't communicate well with others. And his tantrums are not like normal tantrums; they're meltdowns that will eventually make regular schooling—and day-to-day life—impossible. Both the prose book, intended for parents, educators, and mental health professionals, and the comic for the kids themselves demonstrate that the journey toward hope isn't simple . . . but with the right tools and teammates, it's possible.

MELTDOWN

ASPERGER'S DISORDER,
CHALLENGING BEHAVIOR,
AND A FAMILY'S JOURNEY
TOWARD HOPE

MELTING DOWN

A COMIC FOR KIDS WITH
ASPERGER'S DISORDER AND
CHALLENGING BEHAVIOR

AUTISM SPECTRUM DISORDER

Mr. Incredible shares the fictional story of Adam, a boy diagnosed with autistic disorder. On Adam's first birthday, his mother recognizes that something is different about him: he recoils from the touch of his family, preferring to accept physical contact only in the cool water of the family's pool. As Adam grows older, he avoids eye contact, is largely nonverbal, and has very specific ways of getting through the day; when those habits are disrupted, intense meltdowns and self-harmful behavior follow. From seeking a diagnosis to advocating for special education services, from keeping Adam safe to discovering his strengths, his family becomes his biggest champion. The journey to realizing Adam's potential isn't easy, but with hope, love, and the right tools and teammates, they find that Adam truly is *Mr. Incredible*. The companion comic in this series, inspired by social stories, offers an innovative, dynamic way to guide children—and parents, educators, and caregivers—through some of the daily struggles experienced by those with autism.

MR. INCREDIBLE

A STORY ABOUT AUTISM,
OVERCOMING CHALLENGING
BEHAVIOR, AND A FAMILY'S FIGHT
FOR SPECIAL EDUCATION RIGHTS

MR. INCREDIBLE

CHILDREN'S COMIC BOOK

*Also look for books on bullying and
Prader-Willi syndrome coming soon!*

CPSIA information can be obtained at www.ICGtesting.com
Printed in the USA
LVOW061130270513

335285LV00001BA/1/P